GOURMET RECIPES FROM A HIGHLAND HOTEL

GOURMET RECIPES FROM A HIGHLAND HOTEL

ERRATUM

Page 17: 6. Gnocchi, line 6, between 'add' and '$2\frac{1}{2}$ oz.' insert '5 eggs, one at a time, beating well, followed by'. This sentence should read: 'Then add 5 eggs, one at a time, beating well, followed by $2\frac{1}{2}$ oz. grated cheese and a pinch of Cayenne pepper.'

by the same author

HORS D'OEUVRE AND COLD TABLE

GOURMET RECIPES FROM A HIGHLAND HOTEL

WILLIAM HEPTINSTALL

FABER AND FABER
24 Russell Square
London

First published in mcmlxvii
by Faber and Faber Limited
24 Russell Square London WC1
Printed in Great Britain by
Latimer Trend & Co Ltd Plymouth

To all who through the years came to learn and without whose help the work done and the dishes created would not have been possible.

W.H.

CONTENTS

ILLUSTRATIONS

AUTHOR'S NOTE

This book is an attempt to answer some of the many queries put to me during my thirty-five years at Fortingall Hotel. I am not now speaking of my staff—the learner cooks had all the information they wished—but of the many guests who would say, 'How do you make . . .' or, 'Will you give me your recipe for . . .' One lady came down to the kitchen in her bedroom slippers every morning for a week to find out how we made the breakfast baps and wholemeal rolls. Another asked to be shown how to make an omelette, which she did very creditably; and years later she told me that on this slender foundation she had been prompted to build what had become a very successful catering venture.

This, therefore, is the fulfilment of a promise made to guests—and to my apprentices alike—that some day I would collect my notes on the dishes which I believed to have been most enjoyed.

I should say that this is not a volume of precise recipes, giving every detail of oven heats and cooking times. It is for people who already know about good food and cooking; though there is a very full glossary for the assistance of those who are not professional chefs. I insist, for instance, on using the word salamander for the incorrectly named gas or electric grill. **I have thought it best in most cases to give the quantities actually used in my kitchen, so that I may pass on what I can to other hoteliers or restaurateurs. It should not be difficult for private persons to adjust the dishes to their own needs.**

I hope that this book will reach many of my old friends from Fortingall. If the recipe or method you seek does not appear, you must forgive me. There were too many for all to be included.

HORS D'OEUVRE

We will begin with hors d'oeuvre as every meal should—something not to detract from the chef d'oeuvre to follow, something to occupy our attention until the late guests are assembled. If there are no late guests, they still give time for the kitchen to get into its stride. As I have already given some 800 hors d'oeuvre, hot and cold, in my former book, I must restrict myself to a few recent creations together with some favourites which I feel cannot be left out.

1 Pissaladière

It is customary in Mediterannean France to beg a handful of bread dough from the village baker as a foundation for this dish; but as bakers no longer bake bread, but merely sell the product of the large machine installations, I suggest you make a pastry of flour and oil as was practised formerly.

Take 1 lb. flour, 6 oz. olive oil, a good pinch of salt and $\frac{1}{3}$ pint water, and make into a dough. Roll out sufficient of this into a rectangle 12 in. × 18 in. on your baking sheet and cover it with thinly sliced onions which have been allowed to fall in oil (see Glossary). Do not allow them to take colour. Arrange a latticework of fillets of anchovies, trimmed to the thickness of a match, put a few black olives here and there and bake in a moderate oven until the base is firm as for pastry.

2 Flan aux Poireaux

Make a flan case in a flan ring of 9-in. diameter. As usual line with paper and fill with white haricot beans or sea-shells or crusts of bread. Then bake and when cool remove the temporary filling. Meantime cut the leeks, with a good mixture of the light green parts, into small pieces and allow them to fall in butter. Then season.

You have now the choice of two alternatives. Either make a custard of 4 eggs to 1 pint of milk or a creamy sauce with extra yolks of egg. Mix with the cooked leeks and fill into the baked flan case. Sprinkle with grated cheese and return to the oven, either to cook the custard or in the second case to brown. This size of flan ring will yield eight generous portions.

3 Beignets Béatrice

Take about 2 tablespoons of prepared pâte à choux mixture, as given in the recipe for gnocchi. Add to it a heaped tablespoon of strip or filleted almonds (the latter for preference, as they are cut by hand and are thinner than the machine-cut strip), together with the same volume of cold cooked ham cut into small dice. Mix intimately and season with salt and Cayenne pepper or Tabasco. Drop teaspoonsful of this mix into deep fat and when they are cooked drain them on absorbent paper. Dish up a pile for service, allowing about six for each guest.

4 Pizza

Pizza is best made in a long strip of puff pastry about 4½ in. wide. When you have extended this on your baking sheet, depress the centre giving a raised border. I suggest this in place of the usual flan, as triangular pieces may be cut from it which will have all the appearance of those cut from a circular flan with much saving of work. For the fillings, chop onions finely with a small proportion of garlic and allow to fall in olive oil. When cool spread on the strip of puff pastry and sprinkle on finely chopped mushrooms and anchovy fillets. Surmount this with a well-reduced stew of tomatoes and pimentos, sprinkle with Mozarella cheese and bake in a hot oven.

Preparing to dish up a Poulet en Cocotte

A leg has been removed, which will be separated into leg and thigh. The other leg will be cut in the same way. The two wing portions will then be removed and the breast cut into two, giving four portions—a piece of leg or thigh with a piece of 'white' meat. Turned carrots, potatoes, turnips and onion are shown with green peas and a tinned copper cocotte ready to receive the bird when carved. The gravy is not shown.

5 Pizzetti

These are smaller editions of the above. They are made in 3-in. patty pans, which you line with rounds of puff pastry cut with a crimped cutter. Press out well with your thumbs at the bottom and then proceed with the filling as above.

6 Gnocchi

There are many ways of making these, but I advise you to use a pâte à choux as your basis. Put on to boil ½ pint milk with 5 oz. margarine. When the fat is melted and the whole boiling merrily, remove from the fire and stir in rapidly 5 oz. flour. Return to the stove for a minute or two to gelatinize the flour, stirring briskly the while. Then add 2½ oz. grated cheese and a pinch of Cayenne pepper.

Pipe the gnocchi out from a Savoy bag with a ¾-in. plain tube into a pan of near boiling, salted water, cutting them off from the end of the tube with a small knife. You should make them not more than ¾ in. long. When they are poached lift them out with a skimmer and place them in soufflé moulds, dusting them with more grated cheese as you do so. Bake and gratinate in a hot oven. You will probably find that they will tend to souffler slightly, so be careful of your timing.

7 Gnocchi alla Toscana

As above, but give your mix a light pinkish tinge with concentrated tomato purée. Sauce the dish over with tomato sauce before gratinating.

8 Gnocchi Verde alla Bolognese

Proceed as before but this time add some well-reduced spinach purée. When dishing up your gnocchi add a spoonful or two of *ius de veau lié.*

9 Chachouka

A North African dish composed of thinly sliced onions, tomatoes and red or green pimentos in roughly equal proportions. Season with salt and Cayenne pepper. Allow to fall in oil; then dish up on round oven-ware dishes leaving a depression in the middle of each into which you break an egg. Bake in the oven until the egg is cooked. Alternatively use lightly scrambled egg and stir in with a skewer.

10 Ratatouille Niçoise

This consists of thinly-sliced onions with a proportion of garlic, sliced de-seeded poivrons, skinned tomatoes and aubergines also sliced. The whole is cooked in olive oil and seasoned with salt and Cayenne.

11 Quiche à L'Espagnole

Use a cooked flan case and spread the interior with a mixture of finely sliced onions with a little garlic, cooked together without colour in olive oil. Over this arrange a layer of strips of cooked red pimento (the canned pimento is useful here). Cover with a nearly-set savoury custard made of 4 eggs to a pint of milk, seasoned with salt and pepper. On the surface arrange a ring of thin tomato slices of even size and sprinkle with grated cheese. Return the flan to the oven to set the custard.

12 Flan Ecossaise

Fill a pre-cooked flan case with savoury custard as above and push into it some debris of smoked salmon cut into strips or broken into small pieces. Sprinkle the top surface with grated cheese and finish baking. Beware of adding salt to your custard mix, as the smoked salmon will furnish all that is necessary.

AVOCADO DISHES

13 As a cocktail

Remove the flesh from an avocado and cut it into small pieces. Season with tomato juice, lemon juice, salt and Tabasco pepper. Chill and either return to the empty skins or serve in cocktail glasses.

14 Avocado fruit salad

Cubes, balls or pieces of avocado flesh may be mixed into an ordinary fruit salad suitably chilled. Or a special salad may be tried by mixing together avocado flesh, small cubes of pineapple, the same of orange flesh and a few black grapes. Season with a spoonful of Cointreau and chill well.

15 Avocado as a sandwich

Use slices of peeled avocado with cold cooked bacon on pumpernickel spread with cream cheese. Alternately a slice of strong cheese may be partnered by sliced avocado and mounted on black bread with cream cheese.

16 Avocado aux Crèvettes

Cut an avocado in half, remove the stone, enlarge the cavity slightly and fill it with a mayonnaise of peeled shrimps or prawns. Heighten the seasoning carefully with Tabasco pepper and a little lemon juice. Dust a little paprika on the top surface.

17 Avocado en Croûtes

Add to the debris obtained from the above the flesh from another half avocado and make a purée by crushing it with the flat of a knife on your slab. Bind with very stiff mayonnaise. Add a mere sprinkling of finely chopped onion, a little chopped white of celery and some very finely shredded green pepper.

Use this to garnish some dried croûtons at the last moment piling up the mixture in the centre and smoothing the sides with a palette knife. A little of the shredded green pepper may be used as a decorative touch. Alternatively shapes baked in small tartlette or boat-shaped patty pans may be used in place of croûtons; but they must be very dry and filled at the last moment or they will become soggy. If pastry boats are used, a peeled prawn may be put at each end.

SOUPS

CLEAR SOUPS

18 Consommé Nature

This can only be made on a large scale. It requires two days to make. The first day a stock is made which is clarified and reinforced on the morrow. For your stock the pot is filled with about 3 gallons of cold water for the quantities given, and 10 lb. fresh beef bones chopped into small pieces. These should first have been blanched by being brought to the boil from cold to remove any suspicion of taint, then refreshed under running cold water.

The garnish for this quantity is 2½ lb. carrots, well scrubbed and cut into four lengthwise, 1¾ lb. white turnips, also cut into four, 1 sliced parsnip, 2 or 3 branches of celery and 1 onion brulé (i.e. put into the kitchen stove until the outside is charred, or cut into halves and the cut sides placed downwards on the hotplate of an electric stove). This gives colour and a wonderful flavour to the resultant stock; 3 or 4 cloves may be stuck into the onion and a clove or two of crushed garlic added. About 1 lb. of leeks, which have been cut into halves lengthwise and well washed to remove any hidden soil, should now be put into the stock together with a handful of coarse salt and a spoonful of crushed peppercorns. Lastly tie a shin of beef with string, as for a galantine, and also a quarter of a white cabbage; and immerse these in your stockpot. They should both be removed when cooked. There are many uses for this beef.

The stockpot should have about 12 hours of slow cooking, except for the shin of beef and the cabbage withdrawn earlier. The next morning this stock is put on to boil at about 8 a.m. and the clarification added 1 hour later. This consists of shin and trimmings of beef which have been passed through the mincer, mixed with surplus whites of eggs and sufficient cold water to make a sloppy mixture. Carrots, turnips, leeks and a branch of celery are cut small and added to the mass stirred into the stock. At this moment any roast beef bones or chicken carcases left from the previous night may be added, care being taken that all is perfectly sound and free from the slightest taint.

The consommé nature will boil till about 11 o'clock but should not yet be skimmed. Turn down the gas, or pull to the side of the stove; so that the pot keeps simmering steadily till noon. By this time the coagulated albumen, which should have risen to the surface as a thick scum, will have sunk again leaving the fat on the surface. This may now be removed by means of a skimming spoon. The heat is turned off or the pot pulled away from the heat. After the consommé has had a few minutes to settle—aided by the addition of 1 pint cold water—a piece of fine linen should be placed over a pointed strainer and the soup run off steadily into bains maries ready for serving.

When the pot is drained it is filled up again with cold water and set to boil. The *fond blanc* so obtained is used next day for thick soups. As for the remnants in the stockpot, if there is any extractable gelatinous matter left in the bones either add them to the next stockpot, or boil them separately and add the stock obtained to the reduction glaze.

19 Pot-au-Feu

Take as a base the consommé nature made yesterday and add to it a garnish of turned carrot and turnip (i.e. little six-sided barrel-shaped pieces about 1 in. in length), pieces of leek of the same length and cut into four and celery also cut into 1-in. lengths. 1-in. cubes of the shin of beef and cabbage removed from the stockpot are added to the Pot-au-Feu and to the Croûte au Pot.

You should allow six pieces of turned carrot, six of the boiled cabbage cubes, four of turnip, an equivalent amount of leek, three pieces of celery and two pieces of beef per person.

20 Croûte au Pot

Add to the above some crusts of small French rolls or *flutes*, cut neatly into triangular shapes with the crust brushed with fat from the stockpot. In fact these soups must have *des yeux dessus*—little globules of fat floating on the surface.

21 Petite Marmite

This should have a flavour of boiled fowl. I recommend the cooking of legs of fowl in the marmite. When they are cooked, take the bone from the thighs and cut the meat into about four suitable pieces, but merely cut the legs across in two. Add these to the Petite Marmite with the rest of the garnish.

These three soups are all served, or should be, in earthenware marmites; and it is a great joy to enter a large kitchen and see at the soup-cook's end of the stove a dozen or more marmites—two portion or four portion—boiling sedately. One feels that here at least the tradition of *la grande cuisine Française* will not be debased.

22 Consommé Madrilène

This is really a clear tomato soup, but it is rarely met as most cooks add a few pieces of tomato flesh to a consommé nature as a garnish.

When next you prepare a clarification, take out a quart or two before it boils and add 6 large ripe tomatoes per quart. Crush or cut them up and allow the consommé to clarify in the ordinary way, with the addition of a *pointe de cayenne*. The garnish for this soup, which is usually served cold, is dice of tomato flesh and/or cooked red pimento. It is also excellent if served hot.

23 Bortsch Polonaise

Take the stock made as usual the previous day, and in addition to the clarifying meat and vegetables add a mirepoix of onions, beetroot and cabbage. Finish as usual. The garnish consists of grated raw beetroot, which is pressed in a cloth to yield the juice, together with a julienne of leeks and the trimmings of roast duck carcasses cut into julienne. The duck bones should have gone into the clarification; but never use any that have had contact with sage. Duck and beetroot are the predominant flavours in a Bortsch.

The Bortsch is served with the beetroot juice and a sauceboat of sour cream. You will also require some piroschki to serve at the same time. These have been fully dealt with in my book *Hors d'Oeuvre and Cold Table*. I usually make them from puff pastry rolled out thinly but an interesting variety can be made with ravioli paste.

24 *Piroschki*

Take a thin sheet of puff pastry (or ravioli paste) and on half of it place tiny heaps of stuffing, which may be cooked fish, meat or vegetable bound with a suitable sauce. Cover with the other half and seal between the heaps, then cut with a knife or small cutter. It is advisable to eggwash the upper layer. You can distinguish between different varieties by keeping them in varied shapes.

Poach the piroschki carefully in near boiling water. If the water boils you will lose the stuffing from many of them!

25 Soupe à l'Oignon Gratinée

Allow a large onion per plate. Slice finely, then cook slowly in a little beef fat in a covered pan, stirring occasionally with a wooden spoon to prevent the contents from frying or taking more than a blond colour. Add sufficient second stock (fond blanc) or water to give the consistency of thin porridge. Next cut as many ½-in. thick slices of bread as required and toast them. Then pile grated cheese on each, roughly ½ in. in thickness, place under the griller to allow the cheese to shrink, melt slightly and finally brown. Put one of these slices of bread in each soup plate, cover with a ladleful of soup, sprinkle with more grated cheese and gratinate.

26 Minestrone

All the vegetables in season may go into this most accommodating of soups, plus rice and macaroni or spaghetti (the latter for preference as it is more easily broken in a cloth against the edge of the table). Use fond blanc or plain water as a foundation, with the addition of some finely chopped or grated salt pork. When it boils throw in the spaghetti and rice followed by finely chopped onion and garlic. Thereafter add carrot, turnip, leeks, the heart of a small cabbage, a potato and any other vegetables all cut into small pieces. Have ready some peeled de-pipped tomatoes cut into convenient-sized pieces and add them to the soup for a final boil. At the last moment throw in a spoonful of chervil or, failing that, of parsley.

27 Mille Fanti

This is a soup which is cleared by its own garniture. Take 2 quarts of stock and add to it a mixture made of 2 oz. breadcrumbs, 2 oz. dry grated cheese and a flavouring of grated nutmeg. (The breadcrumbs may be of dried bread crusts and the cheese of rinds, finely ground.) The whole is mixed with a whole egg and, if this is not sufficient to make a 'pourable' paste, add a spoonful or two of the stock to make it so.

When the bulk of the stock is boiling, add the mixture stirring briskly, and remove from the fire. You will find that the soup has cleared leaving a crumb-like garniture, and except for rectification of the seasoning it will be ready for service.

28 Consommé aux Oeufs Filés

For a gallon of soup, 2 eggs will be sufficient. Mix whites and yolks together as intimately as possible, season them with salt and pepper and do not make any more froth than can be avoided. Have the soup boiling in a shallow pan on the stove and draw it to the side so that it comes just off the boil. Tip the beaten egg into a fine-meshed pointed strainer and promenade this above the surface of the liquid. The cooking is immediate. The soup may now be poured into a bain marie and given a few beats with a whisk to break up the threads of egg somewhat.

29 La Soupe aux Choux

The best cabbage for this soup is the hard white Continental one that is used for making sauerkraut. It does appear on the market sometimes labelled Dutch. It should be sliced thinly on the mandoline and put to cook in water accompanied by a carrot, an onion stuck with 2 cloves and a bouquet garni. A piece of pickled flank of pork should be added (see page 161); but failing that use either a pickled or fresh flank of mutton. This cabbage soup needs long cooking, 4 hours is a minimum. Towards the end of that time, say an hour before serving, a potato cut in a grosse brunoise should be added: this thickens the liquid very slightly.

When I was in Scotland we used to get partridges, some young and some grandfathers. I found that the best way to deal with them was to serve them as Perdreaux aux Choux (see page 73); and if I removed the birds when cooked I could use the surplus cabbage to make a Soupe aux Choux, using slices of cooked carrot and pickled pork as garnish.

30 Poule au Pot Henri IV

Truss an old hen and immerse it in a marmite of good consommé. Cook slowly and you will have an excellent broth if you add some turned vegetables.

The cold cooked fowl may be used in a variety of ways especially if it has been cooked gently. You may wonder what Henry the Fourth of France had to do with boiled fowl. It was he who expressed the wish that France would become so prosperous that every household would have a chicken in the pot every Sunday for lunch; and that was about 1599. There is a famous equestrian statue of him on the Pont Neuf which in spite of its name is the oldest bridge in Paris.

THICK SOUPS

I do not propose to burden you with a repetition of Green Pea, Lentil, Tomato, Potato and the rest—you can probably make them as well as I—but to offer you some variations of these which were popular with the guests at my hotel, and others that may be new to you.

31 Potage Bonne-Femme

Slice some leeks and allow them to fall in butter but do not let them take colour. Then add potatoes cut into dice, fond blanc (i.e. second stock), salt and pepper. If the soup is not thick enough a small quantity of potato flour will help, but take care to add it slowly, giving time for it to thicken between additions. Finish by adding cream, top of the milk or canned milk. Verify the seasoning at the end.

32 Crème de Volaille

For this soup use as good a chicken stock as you have available, and thicken with a roux (butter and flour). Finish with cream and a garnish of julienne of chicken.

33 Crème d'Oseille or Potage Santé

Strip the stalks and mid-ribs from the sorrel and cut the green remains of the leaves into a fine julienne. Cook this in butter and add it to a crème de volaille, made as above but without the garnish of chicken julienne.

34 Crème Dubarry

Take some of the water used for cooking a cauliflower and cook in it sufficient of the stalks and mid-ribs of the tender leaves to make a purèe when passed through a sieve. Add the purèe to a cream soup and add the flowerets as garnish.

35 Crème de Céleris

Cut tender celery and raw potato into small pieces, in the proportion of seven of the former to three of the latter. Put these on to boil in fond blanc and, when thoroughly cooked, pass them through the soup machine. As a modern alternative to a soup machine use a blender or liquidizer and afterwards sieve if necessary.

Add cream and rectify the seasoning. Serve with croûtons as garnish.

36 Crème Carmen

To a good cream of chicken soup add dice of canned red Spanish pimento. Some cooks colour this soup a very pale pink —a mere suggestion of pink—with concentrated tomato purée. This was a very popular soup at Fortingall Hotel.

37 Cock-a-Leekie

Split the leeks, wash out all the soil and cut them into ½-in. lengths. Put these on to boil in stock, then truss an old hen and immerse it in the liquid. At this stage a handful of dried prunes may be added or not as preferred. When the fowl is cooked, remove it and cut the meat into smallish pieces. These are added to the soup. If they are used, serve a cooked prune in each soup-plate.

38 Scots Broth

If ever you have a boiled gigot (i.e. leg) of mutton with vegetables, do not lose the opportunity of having Scots Broth made with the bree or broth on the next day. All you have to do is to strain off the bree and when it is boiling add a cupful of pot barley followed by carrots, turnips, leeks, celery and onions cut into dice. Some add green cabbage leaves cut into squares of the same size. Boil gently until the barley and vegetables are cooked and add dice of the cooked mutton. A handful of chopped parlsey is an improvement.

If there is any doubt about this soup being thick enough, a small quantity of barley flour mixed into a cream with cold milk and whisked into the boiling soup will remedy matters.

EGG DISHES

OMELETTES

39 Omelette Nature

It is very difficult to explain how to make an omelette, but easy to demonstrate the process. First acquire if possible *une poêle à omelette*. The lip of this pan is curved in both horizontal and vertical senses. Break two eggs into a basin, season with a pinch of salt and a turn of pepper from the pepper mill (do not use ground pepper). Using a fork beat the yolks and whites together but do not attempt to beat any air into the mix, merely amalgamate the two.

Meanwhile the omelette pan should have been heating up on the stove with a pat of butter in it. Now increase the heat and turn in the beaten eggs, stirring vigorously until the eggs begin to set. Then tilt the pan slightly away from you and roll the set egg in the same direction. Pass the fork round the lip of the pan and with your fist give the handle of the pan a blow which will cause the omelette to make a slight jump. Next take the service dish in your left hand, bring the lip of the omelette pan to the centre and by a quick movement turn out the omelette on to the dish. I wish I could give you a demonstration at the stove and get you to make one for me there.

40 Omelette aux Fines Herbes

Add to the beaten egg a good pinch of fines herbes (i.e. chopped parsley, chervil, tarragon and chives).

41 Omelette aux Champignons

Slice a mushroom cap thinly and cook the slices in a little butter and add them to your butter in the pan. Turn in your eggs and proceed as usual.

42 Omelette au Jambon

Cut a slice of lean ham into small dice and fry these slightly in bacon fat before making the omelette.

43 Omelette à L'Estragon

This is like one aux Fines Herbes except that you only use chopped tarragon leaves in the mix.

44 Omelette Charcutière

Use dice of cooked belly pork and slices of cooked pork sausage in the omelette mix, which is made as usual.

45 Omelette au fromage

This is made by mixing a small amount of grated Parmesan cheese into the beaten eggs before the omelette is made, and sprinkling the same on the top before it is served.

46 Omelette aux Rognons

Make a plain omelette as usual. When about to serve it, make a slit on the top which you fill with a small stew of sliced sheep's kidneys cooked in butter and finished in brown sauce which you should have hot and ready.

47 Omelette aux Foies de Volaille

This is similar to the last, except that chicken livers take the place of sheep's kidneys.

48 Omelette aux Pointes d'Asperges

A similar omelette to the last. Two-inch lengths of sprue in little bouquets of six (blanched and finished in butter) are placed in the slit.

49 Omelette Paysanne

Take some dice of cooked, salted belly pork and small cubes of potato blanched and cooked in pork fat. Mix these in your eggs for the omelette, with chopped parsley, and proceed as usual.

50 Tortilla Española

This is made as an ordinary omelette but is not folded. The eggs are mixed with dice of cooked vegetables—red pimento, tomato flesh, and onions, with a suspicion of garlic and the addition of chopped chervil and parlsey. Do not fold the omlette but see that it is cooked on both sides. Toss it over.

OEUFS SUR LE PLAT

51 Oeufs sur le plat Nature

These are eggs cooked on an eared porcelain dish. The cooking of an oeuf sur le plat is the supreme test of a cook's skill. The white

top centre: Pissaladière

left: Stuffed avocado *right:* Stuffed avocado

bottom centre: Beignets à la Mathurine

is not overcooked and the yolk raw with a veil of partly-cooked white over it. Sufficient butter must be used to prevent the white from attaching itself to the dish; it should be free at all times. The egg dishes should be heated in the oven, buttered and the eggs broken thereon. Season with pepper and salt and place under the salamander until the yolk begins to take on a milky look. Remove and serve. If there is any garnish or sauce to be added this is the moment for it.

52 Oeufs sur le plat Meyerbeer

Break an egg on to a buttered egg-dish and season. When cooked split a cooked sheep's kidney in half, place the halves on each side of the yolk and run a cordon of sauce Madère round the edge of the dish and over the kidney.

53 Oeufs sur le plat Bercy

As above. This time put half a grilled pork sausage on each side of the dish and use tomato sauce for the cordon.

54 Oeufs au plat Hotelier Suisse

Follow the usual procedure but cover the egg with cream, then put grated cheese over and gratinate slightly.

55 Oeufs au Beurre Noir

Cook the eggs as usual but keep them a little on the underdone side. Season, then make a Beurre Noisette in an omelette pan, and having sprinkled your eggs with French vinegar, cover them with the foaming butter.

56 Oeufs au Plat Forestière

Have ready a little stew of sliced mushrooms in butter. Cover the bottom of the egg-dish with this and proceed as before. A cordon of Sauce Madère may be run around.

OEUFS EN COCOTTE

These are another useful addition to the luncheon carte du jour and do not require a big outlay for special equipment. The actual cocottes are made in oven-proof ware, brown or green on the outside and white on the inside. Those of French make are about 3⅜ in. in diameter and have a handle which is a nuisance as it is the first thing to be broken. The English ones are slightly bigger: about 3½ in. diameter which does not appear much but the capacity is greater. They do not have a handle. It helps service if the cocottes are kept in boiling water on the stove, taking them out as required.

57 Oeufs en cocotte

A little butter is put in the cocotte and the egg broken on to this and seasoned. The cocotte is then put into the oven or under a salamander.

58 Oeufs en cocotte à la crème

Cover the seasoned egg with a spoonful of cream before returning it to oven or salamander.

59 Oeufs en cocotte au jus

Cook the eggs as above, replacing the cream with a good veal stock, well reduced, or a Sauce Madère.

60 Oeufs en cocotte Florentine

Spread the borders of the cocottes with a thin layer of spinach cooked in butter and lightly chopped. Put a small spoonful of cream in the bottom of each and break an egg thereon. Season and cover with cream, sprinkle with parmesan and return to oven or salamander to finish cooking.

61 Oeufs en cocotte Yorkshire

Chop some cooked Yorkshire ham finely, mix it with cream and spread this farce around the edge of each cocotte, leaving room to accommodate an egg. When the egg is cooked, place a round of thinly cut lean ham (about the size of half a crown) on the yolk and surround it with a cordon of jus lié.

62 Oeufs en cocotte aux Crevettes

Put a few peeled shrimp tails into a buttered cocotte and break an egg on to them. Season and cook as outlined above. When serving, place a small heap of shrimp tails in the centre and run a spoonful of melted butter over.

63 Oeufs en cocottes Mexicaine

Slice thinly 1 or 2 pimentos (minus the seeds) and an equal amount of tomatoes (minus both seeds and skins). Now cook in butter a little finely chopped onion with a suspicion of garlic and add the pimento and tomato mix. Place a spoonful of this mixture in the bottom of each cocotte, break an egg on to this and cook in the usual way. The subsequent dressing may be either a cooked mushroom on the yolk or some of the sauce rendered by the pimento, tomato and onions.

FISH

SALMON

Anyone who has run a hotel on a salmon river will agree with me that there is not a fish that can equal the accommodating salmon.

It may be poached, grilled or braised, but NEVER boiled.

64 Method of Poaching a Whole Salmon

If you are cooking a whole fish, or even a large cut, do not allow the cooking liquor to do more than shiver (*frissonner*). To verify whether the fish is cooked or not, lift the bone carefully. If the flesh parts easily from it and has the familiar salmon colour, well and good; but if it has the orange tint of uncooked salmon, return it to the water. Some say 'pull out a fin' but this is too risky.

The debris left after carving a whole fish may be used in a variety of ways, assuming that all bones, scraps of skin and especially scales are carefully removed.

65 Coquilles de Saumon

Use scallop shells, the deep ones naturally. Give them a border of Pommes Duchesse or not as desired, place cooked fish in position and cover with a Sauce Mornay or a Sauce Vin Blanc. Gratinate in the first case and glaze in the latter. The Duchesse potato may not be eaten by your guests, but it does serve to hide the bare shell.

66 Croquettes de Saumon

This is the rich uncle of fish cakes. Take one part of cold cooked salmon and half the amount of cooked mushrooms cut into small dice. Season and bind these with a well-reduced Béchamel sauce, itself bound with 4 yolks to 1 pint. Spread this mixture on a dish and, having brushed the surface with melted butter, allow it to become cold.

Next shape this on a floured table into squares, rounds or ovals about $\frac{1}{2}$ in. in thickness and of a size suitable to your tariff. Egg and breadcrumb, and fry in deep fat. Avoid making your croquettes into the shape of a mutton cutlet; nothing looks more silly, especially if a short length of macaroni is inserted to imitate the bone bearing a cutlet frill!

67 Mousse de Saumon, à ma façon

Select pieces of raw salmon free from skin, scales and scraps of bone. If you are using a piece of tail, see that it is free from the stringy tendons which are found there. Put this into the liquidizer with a white of egg or two and mix until smooth. Then add about as much cream as salmon flesh and season. Using a $\frac{3}{4}$-in. plain tube, pipe out the mousses in the shape of meringue shells on a buttered fish placque. Pour over them either salmon cuisson or plain hot salted water, and poach gently with a sheet of buttered paper over them. To serve, dress the mousses on a fish dish, sauce over with a suitable fish sauce and decorate with blanched tarragon leaves.

68 Brochettes de Saumon à la Fortingall

For this cut cubes of salmon from the shoulder or tail of the fish, measuring about $1\frac{1}{4}$ in. each side. Thread them on skewers alternately with squares of cooked salted belly pork, or squares of streaky bacon. Always start and end with an uncooked mushroom. Brush with melted butter.

For service these are grilled, or better cooked in the oven. A sauceboat of melted butter should be handed with the dish.

69 Escalopes de Saumon Dorothée

Escalopes of uncooked salmon are decorated with alternating slices of tomato and cucumber, say three of the former and two of the latter, and cooked on a buttered placque with white wine. When dished they are sauced over with a Sauce Vin Blanc which may be glazed or not as desired.

70 Grilled Salmon

Half-inch thick slices of salmon are seasoned, dipped in flour and grilled. Then they are served with either Sauce Rémoulade or Sauce Robert.

71 Poached Salmon (in slices or steaks)

Salmon in ½-in. thick slices may also be poached in salted water and served with a plain-boiled potato and Hollandaise Sauce. Or, in the early months of the year, serve with new potatoes, fresh green peas and Parsley Sauce (with sufficient parsley in it to hold the ladle almost upright).

72 Koulibiaka

This is a kind of pie and, though it may be made with meat or the white cabbage used for sauerkraut, it lends itself best to a more elaborate one made with salmon. Cut thin escalopes from the shoulder, belly or tail, give them a touch with the cutlet bat, fry them lightly and reserve. Prepare hard-boiled eggs, chopped or sliced mushrooms and kascha. This last is semolina cooked to a stiff paste in salted water. Lastly there is vesiga, which is the dried spinal marrow of the sturgeon. Vesiga must be soaked in cold water for 6 hours then cooked in salted water until tender. Do not overcook or it will be sticky and useless. Cut or chop it roughly, mix with it a little melted butter and all is ready for assembling the koulibiaka.

Roll out a sheet of puff pastry 12 in. wide by 18 in. long and $\frac{3}{16}$ in. thick. Transfer this to a floured piece of thick cardboard. Spread a layer of kascha in the middle covering an area 10 in. by 5 in. and on this put half your chopped or sliced mushrooms. Over this put sliced hard-boiled egg followed by chopped vesiga and the escalopes of salmon and more vesiga. Complete the filling of the koulibiaka with the remainder of the sliced boiled eggs, mushrooms and kascha.

Cut a strip of puff-pastry 2 in. wide and $\frac{3}{16}$ in. thick, long enough to cover the top of the built-up koulibiaka, place it in position and egg-wash it. Now make four cuts, one at each corner of the original sheet of pastry giving four flaps, fold the long ones on to the strip and seal them to it. Next cut off any surplus pastry from the remaining two flaps and seal them on to those in position either by egg-wash or by pinching.

There is now the problem of transferring the koulibiaka to the baking sheet. You may slide it carefully off the cardboard or, with the help of an assistant, reverse it on to the baking-sheet. The latter method has the advantage that the closings are in the main underneath, but your beautifully arranged filling may be disarranged. Make two holes in the top and, when the koulibiaka has been egg-washed all over and baked, pour in a small amount of melted butter. Some cooks decorate the exterior with scroll work or leaves of pastry. However, as the dish will be served cut into slices of about an inch in thickness, for any but a special meal this appears to be wasted effort.

Koulibiaka may be made quite successfully with a rather stiff brioche dough and is, in fact, more often done that way in Russia, its country of origin. Puff-pastry is easier to handle.

SCAMPI

For general use scampi are best poached in salted water; but in a few cases they may be cooked in the sauce which will accompany them.

73 Scampi Mornay

Cook the scampi as above. Dress the scampi on a fireproof dish with a border of sliced cooked potatoes. Cover them with a cheese sauce, sprinkle them with grated Parmesan cheese and gratinate.

74 Scampi Florentine

Proceed as above but dress the scampi on a bed of leaf spinach, tossed in butter with the addition of a suspicion of nutmeg in the seasoning.

75 Scampi Bonne-Femme

For this variety dress the scampi on a little stew of sliced mushrooms, cover with Sauce Vin Blanc and glaze.

76 Scampi Napolitaine

Prepare spaghetti alla Napolitana, which is spaghetti cooked in salted water, drained and bound with a good tomato sauce and grated Parmesan cheese. Use some of this to carry the scampi, previously poached in tomato sauce. Sprinkle with Parmesan cheese but do not gratinate.

77 Risotto di Scampi

On an earthenware or porcelain dish form a ring of Risotto alla Milanese and fill the centre with scampi which have been cooked in thin tomato sauce. Sprinkle with grated Parmesan cheese.

78 *Risotto alla Milanese*

As rice requires one and a half times to twice its own volume of liquid for cooking, you should always measure your rice and the water or stock by the same measure. Heat half a cup of olive oil and add to it slowly by hand, stirring with a wooden spoon, two cups of washed Italian rice. When the rice is coated with the oil and the grains are free, stir in a large onion finely chopped and continue stirring until the mass assumes a faintly brown tint. Use a moderate heat only. Now add slowly three cups of chicken stock (or failing that water) in which you have mixed a good pinch of saffron. The rice will take about half an hour to cook. Season with salt. Then mix into the still moist rice one cup of grated Parmesan cheese (any mild grated cheese may be substituted). There are some who add sliced mushrooms and tomatoes concassé to this rice, but the recipe given above is a genuine Italian one.

79 Scampi en Pilaff

Prepare a Riz Pilaff as follows. Then take a semi-spherical tin mould and smear it well with butter. On this arrange your decoration, which may be cooked green peas, soaked currants and/or strips or shapes of red pimento. On this arrange a good layer of the pilaff rice and fill the hollow with poached scampi bound with Sauce Vin Blanc, and cover with a layer of rice. At the moment of service reverse this mould on to a dish and surround the pilaff with a cordon of Sauce Vin Blanc. If the proper moulds are not available a basin may be used.

80 *Riz Pilaff*

Decide upon the amount of rice required and measure it. Then chop an onion finely and fry it lightly in oil and add the measured rice. Allow both to cook together for a few minutes then add twice the measured amount of rice in either water or stock and season. Bring to the boil, cover the surface with a greased paper and put on a tightly-fitting lid. Place the pan in the oven and leave it there for 20 minutes.

81 Scampi aux Fines Herbes

Poach the scampi as usual in fish stock or salted water and arrange them on a porcelain egg-dish over a bed of sliced, boiled potatoes, or in an overlapping ring of the same. To cover them use a Sauce Vin Blanc to which has been added some cream and chopped parsley, tarragon and chervil, with a minute proportion of chives. This dish is not gratinated.

SOLE

82 Grilled Sole

Remove black skin and cut the fins well back, head off and tail off. With your filleting knife, ease the fillets slightly on each side of the backbone (this for ease in serving at the table) and break the backbone in two places. Season the fish, brush it with melted butter and dip it in flour. Place it on the grill and I strongly advise you to use a double grill so that the sole may be turned over easily. This applies to gas or electric salamanders (wrongly termed grills) or a true coke or charcoal grill or one of the gas-char grills.

Dish up on a hot silver dish, the border of which you have

decorated with thin slices of notched lemon and small diamond shapes of cooked sliced beetroot or tiny fronds of curly parsley.

83 Fried Sole

Remove head, fins and black skin. Next cut down to the bone on the now skinless side and ease the fillets slightly away from the backbone. This enables the heat to penetrate more easily to the centre of the fish and will help the service at the table later. Season the fish and pass it through flour then beaten egg and finally fine breadcrumbs. Fry in deep fat or preferably oil. Allow to drain for a moment or two. Then dish up on a folded napkin or a dish paper, with a bunch of curly parsley at one end and half a fancy cut lemon at the other.

84 Sole fillets, fried

Remove the four fillets from the sole and take off the skins, otherwise they tend to curl and deform. Fry as before, and send to the table with a bunch of parsley and eighths of lemon as garnish, with a sauce-boat of Tartare or Rémoulade Sauce.

85 Sole en Goujons

Fillet a sole and remove both skins. Then cut each fillet across in a diagonal manner giving about six or seven strips per fillet. Season these and pass them through flour, then well-beaten egg with a little oil in it and of course a pinch of salt, and finally through very fine breadcrumbs. Now roll these under your hand on the table and they are ready for frying in the deep fat. Six of these to a portion will give a good return. Accompaniments: lemon quarters, bouquet of parsley and any of the cold sauces, Tartare, Gribiche, Rémoulade.

86 Filets de Sole Caprice

Season the fillets of sole, dip them in melted butter and then in fine breadcrumbs. Arrange them on a placque and put them under the salamander—they will not take long to cook. Have ready grilled halves or quarters of banana and place one on each fillet. Serve with Sauce Robert.

87 Filets de Sole Meunière

The correct way to prepare this dish is to season the fillets, then pass them through flour, milk and again flour—then cook them in butter. Personally I do not think that anything is lost if they are cooked in shallow oil and, after sprinkling with a few drops of lemon juice, a Beurre Noisette is thrown over them.

88 Filets de Sole Meunière à l'Orange

Proceed as above; but before adding the beurre noisette arrange on the sole some slices of orange peeled to the quick.

89 Filets de Sole aux Piments Rose

This is the same; but strips of cooked red pimento are laid across the fillets. Canned pimento may be used. This is an eye-compelling dish.

90 Filets de Sole Doria

As before, the garnish being little pieces cut from a peeled cucumber with a fancy vegetable scoop and cooked in butter. If no scoop is available, cut small dice.

91 Sole Bonne-Femme

Butter a plat à poisson and sprinkle on it chopped shallot (or failing that very finely chopped onion but half the quantity), thinly sliced mushrooms and chopped parsley. On this place the trimmed sole, pour on it a glass of white wine and a spoonful or two of fish stock or velouté. Place a well-buttered piece of grease-proof paper over and cook in the oven.

When cooked dress the sole, pour off the liquor into a sauteuse and reduce it quickly. Add a little more stock or velouté and a pat of butter if required. Sauce the fish over with this and glaze under the salamander.

92 Filets de Sole Bonne-Femme

The procedure is somewhat different. Cook the fillets in either fish stock or salted water. The liquid must be kept below boiling or the fillets will roll up or twist like corkscrews. Have ready some sliced mushrooms cooked with chopped shallots in butter. Also prepare a good fish sauce bound with yolks of eggs and finished with butter.

To dress, smear the dish with butter or run a thin film of the sauce over it, then arrange the fillets of sole alongside one another, sprinkle them with the cooked sliced mushrooms, dust a little chopped parsley over and sauce them. Glaze the dish under the salamander.

93 Filets de Sole Véronique

Remove the fillets from a sole, skin them, flatten them slightly with a cutlet bat and fold them. Arrange them on a buttered plaque and sprinkle some white wine over them. Allow them to rest for a few minutes. Then add fish stock, place a buttered paper over and cook in a hot oven. Reduce the cooking liquor almost to nothing, whisk in some fish velouté and a spoonful of cream. Arrange the fillets of sole on the service dish tails to centre and sauce them over. The garnish consists of peeled and de-pipped muscat grapes, heaped in the middle of the dish. If individual portions are being dressed a neat little pile of four grapes with one on top, placed on the fish, suffices.

As it is a messy and time-consuming job to peel grapes I advise you to buy Spanish peeled grapes in cans; but you will have to remove the pips yourself. This is how you do it. Take a piece of thin wire about 2½ in. long and bend it back on itself in the middle. Now push the ends of the wire into a cork and give the doubled piece the outline of a spoon by bending it slightly. With this little tool you will be able to eject the pips quite easily.

TROUT

94 Truite Meunière

For individual service select trout of about 6 oz. in weight and bone them. This is best done by removing the head, cutting the skin down the back, then grasping the backbone between thumb and forefinger of one hand and running those of the other hand alongside the bone from head to tail. Snap off the bone at the tail end and remove dorsal and ventral fins.

Open out the fish and season the interior with salt, pass it through flour and sauté in oil. Dish up on a hot dish, squeeze a few drops of lemon juice on it and throw a little chopped parsley, then a beurre noisette over.

95 Truite Grenobloise

Proceed as for Truite Meunière, and when the fish is cooked and on the service dish, arrange on top a few slices from a lemon which has been peeled to the quick; together with a teaspoonful of capers, a good pinch of coarsely chopped parsley and lastly a beurre noisette.

96 Truite aux Epinards

Have ready some épinards en branches sauté au buerre, which consists of spinach stripped of centre stalks, washed in plenty of cold water and cooked in a minimum of salted boiling water, then drained, pressed and sautéd in butter.

Use small trout. Keep them whole, gut them, trim off the fins, shorten tails and cut about six notches on each side (in culinary terms *ciseler*). Season, flour and cook them in shallow oil, or in other words sauté à l'huile. Dress them on an oval-shaped bed of the leaf spinach, squeeze a few drops of lemon juice over them and throw a beurre noisette on top.

97 Truites aux Amandes

For this you use fillets from a larger trout, say an 8- or 9-oz. fish. Cook them in the usual way à la meunière and, when you have dished them, sprinkle on them a few filleted almonds that you have carefully browned a little under the salamander. There is nothing easier to burn than almonds, so do not take your eyes off them for a second. Finish with a beurre noisette as usual.

98 Truite à l'Américaine

This is a manner of serving trout when you have some left-over sauce from Lobster Américaine. It is more than likely that the sauce will be too stiff to be workable, but a few spots of tomato juice will put matters to rights. If you are really à court with the sauce, then it is best to prepare an imitation one. Chop an onion finely and cut a carrot into a fine brunoise. Fry these in a mixture of half butter and half oil, but do not allow them to take any colour. Blaze with a glass of brandy and add 4 skinned and de-pipped tomatoes roughly chopped, ½ pint of good fish stock and a ¼ pint vin blanc, a spoonful or two of tomato sauce and a knob of fish glaze. Reduce this over a brisk fire then add a spoonful of chopped parsley.

top centre:
Halibut Boulangère

top left:
Escalope de Saumon Dorothée

top right:
Brochettes de Saumon à ma façon

centre:
Risotto di Scampi

bottom left:
Avocado aux crevettes

bottom right:
Avocado aux crevettes

For this dish use one fillet from an 8-oz. trout per person, place it on a buttered earthenware dish, coat it with the sauce, place a buttered paper over and cook in a hot oven.

99 Filets de Truite Alsacienne

Take the two fillets from an 8-oz. trout. Place some cooked or canned sauerkraut as a bed on an earthenware oven dish and arrange the fillets upon it. Put a long slice from a pickled gherkin on each fillet and coat the fish with cream thinned with sauerkraut juice. Cook in the oven.

HALIBUT

100 Halibut au Vin Blanc

Cut off the head of the halibut then halve the fish by sawing along the backbone from the tail. Wash the fish and cut into steaks (or call them cutlets, if you prefer), which may be for two portions at the shoulder end, diminishing to single portions at the tail. Put to cook in a buttered sole dish, whether bi-metal or earthenware. Season and pour into the dish—to half the height of the fish only—a mixture of $\frac{1}{3}$ vin blanc to $\frac{2}{3}$ fish stock made from the head, fins and tail of the halibut. Do not cover the fish with the stock, for if you are using a really fresh fish there will be a curd form on the exposed surface and you may be entertaining a gourmet at your table, who will award you full marks. Do not use a cheap white wine or the stock will take on a nasty grey colour. Place a thickly buttered paper over the fish and cook in a hot oven.

With the cooking liquor prepare a Sauce Vin Blanc. This may be served apart, in which case you should arrange a few neatly turned plain-boiled potatoes around the fish with a bouquet of parsley at one end, and offer a sauce-boat of the sauce.

An alternative way to serve this dish is to coat the fish with a well-reduced sauce bound with a yolk of egg and glaze under the salamander.

101 Halibut Boulangère

Arrange a border of overlapping slices of cold boiled potato around the edge of an earthenware fish dish and butter the bottom well. On this place a slice or slices of halibut and season. Add further pats of butter to the fish and a small quantity of fish stock to prevent drying out, place a buttered paper on top and cook in the oven.

Have ready some very finely chopped parsley mixed with some equally finely chopped garlic, but only enough to give a hint of its presence. On removing the dish from the oven spread a little of this mix on top and sprinkle a pinch of dried breadcrumbs over. This is a dish which requires plenty of butter.

102 Halibut Portugaise

Make a *Sauce Portugaise* by chopping finely 2 medium-sized onions and 1 clove of garlic crushed before chopping. Allow these to fry gently in oil and meantime skin, de-pip and chop roughly 1½ lb. of ripe tomatoes. As soon as the onions show signs of taking colour, add the tomatoes and any juice that the pips may yield when pressed in a pointed strainer. Season with salt and pepper. To counteract any acidity in the tomatoes a teaspoonful of sugar may be added at this stage.

Butter the service dishes and arrange the portions of halibut on this as required, then coat the fish liberally with sauce. Cover with a buttered greaseproof paper, cook in the oven and on withdrawing sprinkle the fish with chopped parsley.

103 Halibut Courgette

If you are unable to get true courgettes, you may substitute small marrows—about 6 to 9 in. in length, but see that they are young enough not to need either peeling or de-seeding. Slice them across thinly and add to them half their volume in tomates concassées (i.e. skinned, seeded and coarsely chopped). Cook this mixture in a buttered pan, season, then spread over the halibut in shallow ovenware dishes which may go to table. Finally place these in a fairly hot oven to cook the fish.

MUSSELS

104 Moules en Brochettes

Prepare for each skewer 6 poached mussels (select large ones), 2 small cooked mushroom caps and two pieces of 1¼-in. square × ¼-in. thick of cooked salt belly pork (or the equivalent in two or three folds of streaky bacon minus rind). Thread these on stainless steel skewers in this order: mushroom cap, 2 mussels, piece of belly pork, 2 mussels, piece of belly pork, 2 mussels and a mushroom cap to complete. Dip these skewers in melted butter and in fresh breadcrumbs, then brown under the salamander. Serve with a suitable sauce or with melted butter.

An alternative way of finishing the skewers is to cover them with a Sauce Vin Blanc bound with yolks and cream, then glaze. If the sauce has sufficient body to set when cold, coat the dressed skewers with it and allow them to set. They may then be dipped into a light frying batter or be egg and breadcrumbed and fried in deep fat. This is known as *Brochettes de moules à la Villeroi.*

MEAT

BEEF

105 A Manner of dealing with a Sirloin

Buy your sirloins regularly and hang them in a fly-proof larder from 7 to 14 days, according to the weather. Do not roast them as sirloins but deal with them as follows. Remove the bone and detach both undercut and flap. You have now three pieces. The first is the topside or contrefilet which you will use as entrecôtes, cutting them in ½-in. slices per portion. (You must first remove the 2-in. strip of gristle which runs under the fat for the whole length, or the entrecôtes will tend to deform during grilling.) Secondly, there is the fillet or undercut which reserve for your best customers, or keep in the refrigerator until you have collected sufficient for tournedos to appear on the table d'hote menu. Lastly there is the flap. (The bone, gristle and trimmings go into the stockpot.)

106 Entrecôte Mirabeau

Cut the entrecôtes from the top-side of a sirloin and grill them. Arrange a lattic-work of trimmed fillets of anchovy along the top with a line of stoned olives filled with anchovy butter. Another way is to use for the lattice-work trimmed fillets of anchovy, together with blanched tarragon leaves stripped of the mid-rib. Arrange the stoned olives and pour over a well-buttered anchovy sauce.

107 Entrecôte Minute

Cut the entrecôtes as usual, take away the fat and the small amount of gristle under it. Now beat them out thinly to about twice the original size, season them and pour a thin film of oil on them. Have an electric hot plate large enough to accommodate one if not two of the steaks at a time, clean it with a wire brush, wipe off any dust with a damp cloth and turn up the heat to medium.

When hot enough to cook the meat, lift one of your prepared steaks on a palette knife and reverse it on to the plate—i.e. oiled side down—and immediately press a butcher's steel down hard on it about four times with a space of 2 in. between. This will simulate the marks left on it as if it were actually grilled over a coke fire. Turn it over but do not leave the steak in contact with the hot plate long. It must have some redness in the interior.

108 Tournedos

Remove fat and detach the undercut from a sirloin. With a small sharp knife trim off this the shiny tendon-like skin and, using the back of the knife, mark where you will cut the tournedos gradually increasing the width between the marks as you approach the thin end. You should get six good tournedos and have left the tail of the fillet, which will serve you as escalopes or medaillons with the discreet help of the cutlet bat. Before cutting the tournedos tie them with string. This will hold them together and keep them in a round shape whilst cooking; but do not omit to remove the string before sending the dish to the table. Tournedos are best sauté in a mixture of oil and clarified butter.

109 Tournedos Bouquetière

Cook the tournedos au beurre and dress them on round toasts of the same size. The garniture consists of little heaps of 6 pieces of turned carrot and 6 of turnip of midget size, with a spoonful of Sauce Béarnaise on the tournedos. Serve with Pommes Parisienne.

110 Tournedos Choron

Deal with the tournedos as above. They may be dished up either on toasts or Pommes Anna (made in a layer not more than ½ in. thick and cut out with a round cutter the size of the tournedos). Prepare a *Sauce Choron* by adding to Sauce Béarnaise enough concentrated tomato purée to give it a pink colour. Put a spoonful of this on the tournedos and mount a cooked tomato on top. If the tournedos is dished on toast, then straw potatoes should be used to garnish the dish.

111 Tournedos aux Asperges

The tournedos as before dished on toasts. On top of each place a pile of six 2-in. lengths of asparagus au beurre with two thin crossed pieces of red pimento to imitate the string.

Or, if you can get pointes d'asperges (sprue), have ready pastry tartlets baked blind and arrange in them a neat garnish of the cooked, buttered pointes. Pommes Parmentier are served with this dish.

112 Sauté de Boeuf à la Bourguignonne

For this use the flank or flap cut from the boned sirloin. Remove surplus fat and cut the lean into chunky pieces of 1½ in. sides. Fry these until browned on the outside, either in the rendered fat or in oil, together with one-quarter of the amount in petit salé of same size as the beef (failing this use pickled flank of pork or streaky bacon cut into cubes together with the rind from the piece: these cubes of bacon should be soaked and must be blanched). Sprinkle with flour, stir in and allow to brown slightly. Add one-quarter of the original weight of the meat in button mushrooms and the same amount of small onions or medium-sized ones cut into quarters. Use half brown stock and half red wine to cover the meat and put in 3 or 4 crushed cloves of garlic. Season with salt and pepper from the mill. Bring to the boil, add a little caramel if necessary, and place in a medium hot oven until the meat is cooked.

113 Boeuf en Daube à la Provençale

One of the treasures of the French cuisine. Cut 3 to 3½ lb. of lean beef into large cubes and with the aid of a large larding needle or *lardoir*, pass a lardoon of pork fat through the middle of each. These lardoons measure ½ in. × ½ in. × 3 in. and are previously rolled in a mixture of finely chopped parsley and garlic. The meat is then marinated in a bottle of white wine with the addition of a glass of brandy.

In France this dish is cooked in a fireclay utensil in a slow oven for 6 hours or so. If you have to use a metal casserole see that the lid is a close-fitting one. Whichever you are using load it as follows: a layer of meat followed by a layer of pieces of pickled pork skin about 1 in. square, more meat, then blanched dice of pickled pork. Continue with meat mixed with sliced carrots, chopped onions, 2 or 3 cloves of garlic well chopped, skinned tomatoes roughly chopped, stoned black olives and small mushrooms. Season each layer with a little salt and pepper. Place a bouquet garni in the centre with a little dried orange peel tied in with it. Fill up with the marinade and add stock if necessary. Plaster the joint between lid and casserole with a paste made of flour and water: this is known as *luter*.

On withdrawing the pot from the oven, remove the bouquet garni, take as much fat as possible from the surface of the stew, and rectify the seasoning.

114 Braised Oxtail Paysanne

Cut the oxtails into joints, reserving the last six or so to be used as a garnish in an oxtail soup. Chop the first three or four into two as they are too big to appear otherwise in a portion. The pieces are now blanched and cooled under running water. They are then put on to braise with fat in the oven, accompanied by a garnish of carrots, turnips and onions in quarters. When these begin to show signs of colouring, drain off the fat and cover the meat and garnish with brown stock. Add a small tin of concentrated tomato purée.

Replace the covered pan in the oven until the pieces of oxtail are cooked, then transfer them to another pan. Strain off the cooking liquor and thicken it if necessary with a little arrowroot. The first garnish may be put through the liquidizer and added to the sauce.

Meantime prepare a fresh garnish consisting per portion of 2 pieces of turned carrot 2 in. in length, 2 of turnip, 1 button or small onion and a ball (of golf ball size) of cooked cabbage squeezed in a cloth. Boil this garnish separately, strain and add at the time of dishing up.

Dish the oxtail in earthenware cocottes with the vegetable garnish on top. Sauce over with the reduced and, if necessary, enriched and seasoned sauce.

115 Braised Beef and Vegetables

Choose a convenient compact cut of rump of beef and, using your lardoir, run lengths of larding bacon ½ in. square section completely through the beef in the sense of the grain, spacing them about 1 in. apart around the edge of the piece. A refinement is to macerate the lardoons in a mixture of finely chopped garlic, a ground clove and a few crushed white peppercorns with a little grated nutmeg and a finely chopped shallot; the lot mixed with a spoonful of brandy. The lardoons should be allowed to remain in contact with this overnight.

Having larded your beef, the next job is to brown the exterior before putting it on to braise with a garnish of a large carrot cut into pieces, a large onion stuck with 2 or 3 cloves and a bouquet garni containing a stalk of celery. Add the remains of the maceration, some brown stock and a bottle of white wine (or, as in Normandy, a bottle of good cider), to two-thirds of the height of the meat. Bring to the boil, cover closely and put into a medium oven until cooked. This may take from 2 to 5 hours according to the thickness of the piece.

The garnish to be served with this dish may be turned carrots, turnips and small onions. Also may be used brussels sprouts or other cabbage, cauliflower, celery, a jardinière, napolitaine, nouilles fraîches or macaronis. For the sauce I strongly advise you to remove such things as bouquet garni, pieces of bone, stray twigs of thyme, or an odd bayleaf or any burnt pieces of carrot, etc., left in the garnish in the braisière, and then put the vegetables through the liquidizer. Add this to the braising liquor and you will obtain a sauce of unequalled excellence.

116 Boeuf à la Mode

This does not differ much from the Pièce de Boeuf described above with the exception that red wine is used in the cooking and three split and blanched calves' feet are cooked along with it. At three-quarters cooking time change the beef into a smaller casserole and place around it the blanched and sautéd turned carrots and button onions together with the cooked and boned calves' feet now cut into squares or rectangles. Pour over these the cooking liquor, thickened slightly if necessary with a little arrowroot. Finish cooking under cover, gently.

117 Boeuf au Gros Sel

This is a simple dish of boiled beef with suitable vegetables and served with coarse salt and cornichons.

118 Boeuf Strogonoff

Here is an opportunity for you to use up those ends of fillet of beef which tend to accumulate. You may either cut them into small cubes or into escalopes, which you flatten thinly and then cut into short strips. Cook sufficient thinly sliced onions and sliced mushrooms in butter. Remove these and in the same butter toss the meat, season then add sour cream. Allow this to simmer slowly for 20 minutes, then either add the onions and mushrooms or make them into a purée and stir that into the sauce.

119 Zrazi

A Russian dish using beef and sour cream. Prepare some kascha—which is nothing more than semolina cooked in salted water, but kept on the stiff side. Beat out thinly escalopes of ends of fillet of beef, spread them with kascha mixed with chopped fried onions and roll. Skewer about three or four at a time on to small stainless steel skewers. Brown them in butter and cook slowly in stock. To serve, reduce the stock, thicken slightly, and blend with sour cream (see page 159).

ESCALOPES

120 Escalopes de Chevreuil Badoise

Select and remove a suitable muscle from a leg of venison (there is one of round section). Cut your escalopes from this and flatten them with the cutlet bat. Season and flour them in readiness. When required for service, sauté the escalopes and keep warm. Detach the glaze from the pan with cream and the juice of cooked cherries. Strain this into sufficient Sauce Poivrade (see page 153). At the moment of service, put a smear of this sauce on the entrée dish and arrange your cooked escalopes upon it. The garnish consists of a neat pile of cooked stoned cherries and the whole is sauced with the Sauce Poivrade.

121 Escalopes de chevreuil à ma Façon

Cut, prepare and cook escalopes as above. Have ready a purée of cooked sweet chestnuts and pipe a rosette on each escalope from a star tube. The same sauce as above may be used for the final touch.

122 Escalopes de Veau à ma Façon

Escalopes of veal are beaten out thinly and evenly with the bat, seasoned, floured and sauté in oil. Drain and dish up. Pour away oil and deglacé with red wine. Strew escalopes with soaked sultana raisins. Add cream to deglaçage and heighten the seasoning with a little French mustard. Stir well together and cover the escalopes with this sauce.

123 Escalopes à la Fortingall

For this use any ends of fillet of beef, pork or veal from which you can, by means of the cutlet bat, flatten out an approximate circle 4 in. in diameter. On this spread a thin layer of the mix used for Croque Monsieur, i.e. beaten egg seasoned with a little dry mustard and mixed to spreading consistency with grated cheese. Salt is not required, the cheese will take care of that. Cover this with a thin slice of cold boiled ham. These escalopes should now be dipped in melted butter, then in fine breadcrumbs and arranged on a baking sheet prior to cooking them in the oven.

124 Escalopes à la Duxelles

This is similar to the last. The only difference is that Duxelles purée, bound with a little sausage-meat, is used instead of the egg and cheese mixture for the sandwiching of escalope and ham.

125 *Duxelles*

Any mushroom stalks, peelings, turnings or broken mushrooms are chopped finely. Next put on to cook in oil about a quarter of the weight of chopped mushrooms in a fifty/fifty mixture of chopped onions and shallots. Do not allow them to take on any colour. It will hinder this if, when you go on to add the chopped mushrooms, you throw in any bottoms of white wine you may have. Reduce and add a spoonful each of tomato sauce and sauce demi-glace. Bring to the desired consistency by adding fresh breadcrumbs.

This purée will keep in the refrigerator if covered with an oiled paper, but do not freeze it.

126 Fritti Quanti

These are very small escalopes about the size of an oval which could be covered by two half-crowns laid side by side. A portion therefore will be about four or five of these cut from ends of fillet veal, pork or beef and thinned to a regular thickness with the cutlet bat. Season, flour and sauté them in oil and butter mixed. Toss them in a demi-glace enriched with a spoonful of Madeira. Serve with gaufrette or straw potatoes and a green vegetable.

127 Scaloppine alla Marsala

Take some slices of veal and flatten them out thinly, of a size about 3½ in. across. Season and flour them and cook them in butter gently. Lift them from the pan and keep them warm, then dissolve any caramelized juices with Marsala and add a spoonful of demi-glace sauce. Dress the escalopes of veal on a dish and sauce over with the Marsala sauce.

128 Wiener Schnitzel

Cut and beat out thinly some veal escalopes as above. Season, flour and egg and breadcrumb them. Fry in oil and on each escalope place a slice of peeled and de-pipped lemon dipped in chopped parsley. Surmount by a stoned olive and encircle this with a fillet of anchovy. Pass hard-boiled egg through the sieve and sprinkle some of this together with a squeeze of lemon juice over the schnitzel; then make a beurre noisette and flush this over them. Serve whilst the dish is foaming, with an accompaniment of straw potatoes.

129 Paprika Schnitzel

Cut slices from end pieces of fillet of veal, pork or fillet of beef and beat them out very thinly with a cutlet bat. Season them and dip one side into paprika, then sprinkle with flour and press. Sauté in oil. When all are cooked, pour away the oil and swill the pan with thin cream. Cover the bottom of the service dish with this sauce and arrange the schnitzel thereon. If potatoes are to be served with this dish it is best to serve Pommes Hongroise.

130 *Pommes Hongroise*

'Turn' the potatoes very small or select new ones about the size of a two-shilling piece. Chop an onion very small and put it to fry in oil, but do not allow it to colour. Add paprika, salt and the potatoes, with sufficient water just to cover. Cover with a lid, bring to the boil and cook slowly.

MUTTON

131 Navarin de Mouton Printanier

Use a fore-quarter of mutton or lamb (with or without the shoulder). Cut and trim the cutlets neatly, and deal with the scrag end and neck similarly. To avoid splinters of bone, saw the breast into pieces of about 3 oz. in weight, say 2¼ in. square.

The trimmed fat should be rendered then decanted and used to sauté the pieces of meat, together with 3 onions cut up roughly and an equivalent amount of carrot. This done, pour off some of the fat and sprinkle the meat with flour and a teaspoonful of fine sugar, which you allow to caramelize slightly to give colour to the sauce. Then flood the meat with mutton stock, season, add a crushed clove of garlic, a bouquet garni and a tiny tin of concentrated tomato purée. Cover with a lid and put in the oven for an hour.

At the end of this time change the meat into another casserole and add 3 each of turned carrots and turnips, 2 button onions and 3 turned potatoes per portion. (Note: the portion of meat is one cutlet or equivalent in neck and two pieces of breast per person.) All the vegetables should first be blanched. If the carrots are new, merely scrape them. The turnips should be peeled, but are better turned if they have any signs of that woody layer that young turnips acquire if grown in dry weather or have been too long in growing. Strain the stock over, verify the seasoning and cook slowly under cover in the oven until both meat and garnish are cooked. I am aware that some cook the meat in the sauce and add the cooked vegetable garnish at the end in time for service; but if you will take my advice you will cook the lot together and thus obtain a far finer flavour in your Navarin.

As each service is ready for the dining-room a few cooked green peas should be strewn over it (or, failing peas, lozenge-shaped cuts of cooked haricot verts), with a dusting of chopped parsley as a finishing touch.

132 Grilled Breast of Lamb or Mutton

After the shoulder, cutlets and neck have been disposed of from a fore-quarter of lamb, there is always some meat left adhering to the carcase. (See also the flank of mutton used in Soupe aux Choux, page 26, which can be used similarly.) By a careful use of the saw, this meat can be cut into pieces about 2½ in. square. These should be tied into bundles of three or four and cooked in stock. When cold the bundles should be untied, seasoned and breadcrumbed. They can then be carefully grilled when required for service; so that they are heated through but the crumbs are not burnt. A boat of Tomato, Poivrade, Piquante or other sauce should accompany them.

133 Lambs' Tongues Charcutière

You may be able to buy pickled lambs' tongues if you live in a city, but if not there are excellent canned ones on the market. In the first case you will need to cook them in water, which will help remove some of the salt. Skin, trim and cut them into two lengthwise. Depending on the size, a portion is two or three halves. In the second case, the cans are heated before being opened, which is an economy. Thereafter the treatment follows the same lines. The garnish in both cases is julienne of pickled gherkin. Sauce over with a brown sauce you may have available, enriched if possible with glaze.

134 Gigot de Mouton Boulangère

Prepare a leg of mutton for roasting by inserting 2 or 3 cloves of garlic around the shank bone to perfume the joint. Then put on to roast in the usual way. Meantime slice sufficient potatoes on the mandoline and mix with them one-third or one-quarter of the bulk in thinly sliced onions—the larger proportion for the North of England, the lesser for the South! Season with salt and pepper from the mill and mix well. Place the potatoes and onions in a suitable sized roasting tin with a little stock, lay a greased paper on top and put into the oven to cook.

When the mutton is three-parts cooked, remove the paper from the potatoes and place the meat on a suitable grid over them, to finish cooking. The original roasting tin with a little help from the brown stock will yield sufficient gravy.

135 Noisettes d'Agneau Parisienne

To bone the loin or not depends on your clientele and therefore on the size of noisette expected. If you take out the bone, curl the little bit of flap around and anchor it and the fillet to the chop with a skewer. If however you are dealing with a loin of baby lamb, the chop will be thicker and should be beaten out slightly with the cutlet bat, do not bone. Grill and serve with a green vegetable (haricots verts, petits pois, laitue braisée) and pommes Parisienne. This last is obligatory.

136 Côtes de Mouton Froides en Macédoine

Remove the chine from as many necks of mutton (best end) as required, and trim down the fat a little. Tie these together in pairs and put them on to braise in a good stock. Allow them to cool in the stock, trim well, then cut off the cutlets.

Prepare a Sauce Chaud-Froid Brune and coat the cutlets one side only (all the same side of course) and decorate with a marguerite made from the yolk and white of a hard-boiled egg or with any other decoration you may fancy—tomato skins and cucumber rind make beautiful poppies. Finish with a coat of aspic jelly applied with a brush, and put a cutlet frill on the end of each bone. Arrange a salade de légumes bound with a mayonnaise collée in a pyramid in the centre of a dish and place the cutlets around, overlapping.

137 Côtes de Mouton Suèdoise

Cut, trim, egg and breadcrumb the required number of mutton cutlets. Prepare sufficient mashed potato and add to it one-quarter of its bulk in sieved cooked apple purée plus one-quarter the amount of the apple in finely chopped grated horse-radish. Mix this well together and keep it hot. Sauté the cutlets on both sides in a mixture of oil and butter. Dress a large oval flat with a pile of the potato mixture, smooth the sides and decorate them with a palette knife. Flood the exposed part of the well of the dish with a rich gravy, arrange the cutlets on this leaning against the potato and send to table with more gravy in a sauce-boat. A green vegetable should accompany the dish.

centre: Concombres farcis

left: Côtes de Mouton à la Suèdoise

right: Tomates farcis

bottom centre: Gravy for the Côtes de Mouton

138 Pilaff de Mouton à la Grecque

Prepare a little brown stew of mutton; if you are using cooked meat see that there are not any hard pieces included. Make a *Riz Pilaff* by cooking a finely chopped onion in oil without browning. Add to this ½ pint of rice and stir together. Then add 1 pint of fond blanc, season, cover with a buttered paper and a close-fitting lid. Bring to the boil and place in the oven for 20 minutes. On removing it do not forget to sprinkle some flour on the handles, the lid and the sides of the casserole as a warning to your assistants not to touch with a bare hand.

To mould the pilaff take a semi-spherical mould and grease it liberally with butter. On this place soaked currants, cooked green peas and thin strips of red pimento as a decoration. Now put in a layer of the cooked rice about ¾ in. in thickness, very carefully so as not to disturb the décor. Three parts fill with the mutton and place a layer of the rice over. Now take a round dish large enough to accommodate the open end of the mould, place it in position and with a quick movement reverse the mould on to the dish. A cordon of sauce on the dish around the pilaff is an improvement.

Always remember to take for a pilaff twice the amount of liquor to rice by volume.

139 Pilaff de Mouton à la Turque

Prepare the rice as above, adding a pinch of saffron with the liquid. When the rice is ready, add a well-reduced Fondue de Tomates. To prepare this, chop an onion finely with a clove of garlic and fry in oil without browning. Then add 1 lb. tomatoes, skinned, de-seeded, roughly chopped and reduced.

140 Ris d'Agneau

Lamb's Breads should be dealt with as ris de veau in the initial stages, i.e. soaked in running water, then blanched and picked over diinvidually to remove hairs, fibres and other unwanted bodies.

As with ris de veau, you have the choice of braising ris d'agneau either brown or white. For the former I suggest your sautéing them quickly in butter until they have a brownish tinge, then finishing the cooking in a good brown sauce. For the latter, cook them in a white stock enriched with sliced carrots and onions, a small bouquet garni, a tiny pinch of grated nutmeg and a few crushed peppercorns.

Ris d'agneau are of use in the fillings for Bouchées, Coquilles (with a border of pommes Duchesse), small Croustades or Tartelettes in short pastry which should be baked blind. You can also use them for Dartois. Take rectangles of puff pastry, place filling in centre, egg-wash border and fold over pastry covering the filling, then seal the edges. Egg-wash top surface, prick with a knife, and bake in a hot oven. In all the fillings above, the ris d'agneau are cut into dice as are also the complementary ingredients, such as white chicken meat, ox tongue, cooked flank of pork, mushrooms. They should be bound with a Sauce Suprême.

141 Ris d'Agneau en Brochettes (Grilled)

Thread the lamb's breads on skewers, starting and finishing with a suitably sized mushroom and alternating them with thin slices of cooked flank of pork. Smear the brochettes with well-reduced duxelles (see page 59), brush with melted butter and sprinkle with fine breadcrumbs. As all the ingredients are cooked except perhaps the mushrooms, it will only be necessary to heat the brochettes through, but the breadcrumbs should be browned slightly. Serve with Beurre Maître d'Hotel.

142 Ris d'Agneau en Brochettes (Fried)

Proceed as above, but spread the brochettes with a well-reduced Sauce Villeroi (see page 154). Allow this to set, then egg and breadcrumb them and fry in deep fat. Send to table with Tomato or other suitable sauce.

143 Lancashire Hot Pot

Trim away the fat from a neck of mutton, cut off the cutlets and bone out the scrag, cutting the meat from this into as many chunks as you have cutlets. One cutlet with one piece of meat constitutes a portion. Brown the meat in the fat before putting it in the hot-pot. This may be of the kind shaped like a soup tureen or better, the straight-sided variety, either of which must have a lid.

Slice 2 onions thinly, slice or cut into pieces 6 or 8 mushrooms and brown them all together in the same fat as the meat. Put the onions and mushrooms on top of the meat, slice 3 skinned sheep's kidneys thickly and arrange these overlapping on top of the onions. Season with salt, pepper and a pinch of sugar. Cut about 2 lb. of peeled potatoes into thick slices, season and arrange these overlapping on the sliced kidneys. Next make a roux with part of the fat left from the frying and a heaped tablespoonful of flour. Add about ¾ pint of water or brown stock, bring to the boil dissolving any meat essence there may be on the pan and pour over the potatoes. Put on the lid and into the oven for 2 hours.

I know that the traditional recipe for this dish requires about one and a half to two dozen oysters to be placed under the potatoes. Take my advice and eat your oysters raw before the meal and not as little chunks of rubber in an otherwise good stew. There is, however, one adjunct which is a must, the provision of a dish or glass jar of pickled red cabbage.

CHICKEN

144 Poulet en cocotte Forestière

Roast or braise the chickens as usual. Dress the portions in earthenware cocottes and garnish with mushrooms dipped in chicken fat and cooked in the oven, and also with Pommes

Château. Rinse the roasting pan with a stock made from the giblets to obtain a gravy.

145 Poulet en cocotte Grand'mère

As above, garnish instead with ¾-in. cubes of fried bread, pieces of streaky bacon and Pommes Parmentier.

146 Poulet en cocotte Jardinière

I suppose that the gardener's wife would have access to whatever vegetables were in season, so make use of all that comes to hand.

147 Poulet en cocotte Paysanne

Cook the chicken as before and garnish with young carrots, turnips and onions. Add a few lardoons of pickled flank of pork which have been blanched then fried in their own fat. The carrots and turnips should be peeled then cut across into rounds about ¼ in. thick.

148 Poulet Braisé Alexandra

This is a way of using the remains of cold cooked chicken whether roast, braised or boiled. Remove skin, trim and cut into as chunky pieces as possible, then heat in chicken stock two pieces per portion (one white and one brown). Arrange these on the serving dish surmounted by 3 stalks of cooked asparagus per person. Cover with a chicken sauce finished in cream, sprinkle with grated cheese and gratinate.

Note: A 2–2½ lb. chicken yields 2 pieces leg, 2 pieces thigh, i.e. the 'brown' meat, and 2 wings and 2 pieces of breast, i.e. the 'white' meat. One piece brown and one piece white is reckoned as a portion.

149 Poulet Braisé Brésilienne

For this dish you may use boiled fowl. Prepare a pilaff rice (as on page 65) with chopped onion and chopped red pimento in it. Place a mound of this on the service dish and decorate with strips of cooked, skinned red pimento. Now arrange the portions of skinned fowl on the rice. Sauce over with a chicken sauce, tinted a faint pink with liquidized (or pounded) red pimento, and dusted lightly with chopped parsley.

150 Poussins Grillés

For this use chick-chickens which are suitable as two-portion birds. Remove feet and scaly legs at the joint and with the kitchen scissors cut through the bird on each side of the backbone, which take away. Next with a knife free the ribs on each side of the breast-bone and lift them out. Flatten the carcase with a cutlet bat and, using strong skewers, truss it flat firmly. Brush it with melted butter, season and sprinkle with fine breadcrumbs. I find it best to cook the chickens in the oven and pass them under the grill on demand. Then, having removed the skewers, to cut the birds in two lengthwise. Serve with either melted butter or a good chicken gravy, and offer vegetables.

151 Chicken Pancakes

Prepare a batch of thin pancakes made without sugar from 8 oz. of flour, 2 eggs, pinch salt and 1 pint of milk. This will make 40 pancakes about 5 in. in diameter. They will be usable for some days if kept between two plates and in a cool place.

For the filling make use of all debris of chicken you may have from carcasses, left-over legs, sot-l'y-laisse and so on; but be careful not to include any dried-up pieces. Cut this debris into small dice and bind with a good chicken sauce. Use this to fill the pancakes—two per portion—and fold over each pancake to give a neat rectangular package. Dress these on flats, sauce over with grated Parmesan cheese and gratinate.

152 Bouchées de Volaille

Bake the required number of good-sized bouchées with separate lids, depress the centres and fill with a similar filling to that indicated above. If the bouchées are to be served cold a slightly thinner sauce should be used—a spoonful or two of cream here would be appreciated.

153 Irish Stew of Chicken

I advise you to use an old hen for this dish as present-day chickens lack flavour. Divide the bird into 8 portions, 1 piece of brown meat and 1 piece of white meat per portion; 4 pieces of brown meat can be cut from each of the legs, 2 wings and the remainder of the white meat from the breast cut into 6 pieces give the white. Place this meat in a plat sauté large enough to accommodate it in one layer and cover it with water or chicken stock for it to bathe freely. Season with pepper and salt, add a bouquet garni and 3 stalks of celery cut across very finely. This last gives an indefinable flavour to the stew but is easily overdone. Peel and slice thinly 6 onions and strew them over the chicken, put on the lid and cook the stew very gently for at least 2 hours.

Take some peeled potatoes, trim them down in size to give three per portion and add the trimmings to the chicken to make the sauce. Put the prepared potatoes, with 1 small peeled onion per portion to cook with the stew about 1 hour before service; and have plenty of chopped parsley on hand.

DUCK, GOOSE, GAME

154 Caneton Braisé à l'Orange

Cut out the wish-bones—to facilitate carving later—truss the ducks and proceed to roast or braise them as usual.

With the necks, feet and giblets make a stock which will form the basis of the sauce, which will be a brown sauce with any demi-glace you have to spare. Having decanted the fat from the roasting pans, swill off all the glaze left from the birds and add this to the sauce. If necessary thicken with arrowroot.

Allow 2 oranges for every 6 portions of duck. Remove the zest from the oranges, chop this finely and add to the sauce. Now peel the oranges to the quick and slice them. When you dish up the duck place 2 slices of orange on each portion before saucing.

155 Caneton aux Cerises

Cook, carve and dish up the ducks as above, but place over them about 5 or 6 cooked red cherries per portion. Sauce as above but without the orange zest. Canned cherries are a help.

156 Caneton Nivernaise

Prepare a purée of white turnips with the addition of one-quarter of the bulk in potatoes and bound with cream. From a bag and star tube pipe this purée on to the dish and arrange the portions of duck alongside. Sauce the duck only.

157 Caneton à la Polonaise

This dish was served to many of our Polish allies during the late war. However, no guarantee can be given that the recipe is purely Polish as it was first met in Paris after the Russian revolution, when many cooks from that country drifted there.

Whilst the ducklings are roasting, prepare the cocottes to accommodate them. This you do by chopping finely sufficient shallots—or onions in default—and cooking them in oil without browning. Smear these over the bottoms of the cocottes and arrange on top mushroom caps which have been dipped in oil. Put the cocottes in the oven until the mushrooms are cooked and on withdrawal strew them liberally with sprigs of fresh young fennel. Bring sour cream to the boil and all is ready for the final dishing-up. As the reduction of cream may be tricky, you may thicken with a little arrowroot.

When the moment arrives to dish up, cut the duckling into neat joints and arrange them on the prepared beds in the cocottes. Sauce over with the boiled cream, which should have attained a coating consistency, and sprinkle chopped fennel over. A sauce-boat of duck gravy made from the giblets should accompany this dish.

158 Faisan en Cocotte

Truss a pheasant and cook it in butter in the actual cocotte. Some cooks add a few button onions and others small mushrooms also. In any case strain a ladleful or so of pheasant stock, which of course you will have made from the giblets, neck, etc., over the bird in the cocotte. This will loosen the glaze, which will probably have formed on the bottom and sides. A boat of this gravy, one of bread sauce, a bunch of watercress and either Pommes Chips, Ribbon or Pailles should accompany the dish.

159 Faisan en Cocotte à la Crème

Truss and cook the pheasant as above and after ½ hour pour over it ⅓ pint of cream. Continue the cooking, basting with the cream from time to time until the bird is cooked. Sour cream may be used or a little lemon juice added.

160 Faisan à la Câreme

As above. Garnish the cocotte with braised celery and 20 minutes before taking the casserole from the oven, fasten the lid to the rim of the dish with a luting of flour and water; and return it to the oven to set. The head waiter will see to it that none of this cooked paste is served to the guests.

161 Faisan Souwarow

Truss and roast a pheasant in a casserole as before. Then either cut the bird into joints and put each portion on a croûton which has been covered with a slice of foie gras, and lay a thick slice of truffle on the pheasant. Or else serve the whole bird and surround it with foie gras and truffles cut into dice. In either case a few drops of brandy should be sprinkled over the meat and a small ladleful of rich gravy poured into the cocotte before luting the lid as already explained.

162 Perdreaux aux Choux

Shred sufficient cabbage to give a bed of about 3 in. deep in the pan you are to use for braising the partridges. Place these breast downwards in the cabbage and add carrots cut into four, 2 onions each stuck with 2 cloves and a bouquet garni. Put a piece of pickled pork in the centre of the pan and add stock. When cooked, remove the birds and use the surplus cabbage for a Soupe aux Choux (see page 26).

163 Bigos

This is a Polish dish and may be likened to a terrine of meat and game mixed, cooked in an earthenware receptacle lined with sauerkraut. If you are dealing with uncooked sauerkraut, you will need to wash it in several changes of cold water and to blanch it; but if you buy a 2½ size tin of Dutch sauerkraut you will save yourself the trouble and have by you the necessary amount to make a large casserole.

Begin the filling of the casserole by putting at the bottom a 1-in. layer of sauerkraut into which you have mixed a finely-grated small onion. On this place a layer of cooked meats, e.g. chicken, duck, ends of fillet of beef escaloped and fried lightly, mutton, rounds of skinned cooked pork sausage, salt cooked flank of pork in slices cut into three. Continue the filling with alternate layers of cooked meats and sauerkraut, sprinkling here and there dice of sour apple and lean gammon. Make a small amount of thin sauce from stock, a little sauerkraut liquor, a spoonful of meat glaze and a roux of butter and flour. Pour this into the casserole with a glass of red wine, put on the lid and push the casserole into the oven for 2 hours.

It is said of Bigos that the more it is re-heated the better it is. There is the odd advantage that a few otherwise unwanted legs of cooked poultry may be dropped into the casserole at any time when re-heating.

164 Confit d'Oie

If you have the chance of preserving a goose in its own fat, seize the opportunity; for you will have the means of making one of the finest dishes that France has given to the world.

Clean and singe the goose and draw it carefully, putting all the fat on one side. Cut the bird into ten or more pieces, depending on its size, and rub each with a mixture of a heaped teaspoon of Jamaica pepper crushed (or better, pounded) with a good pinch of rubbed thyme and a tablespoon of coarse salt. Stow away in a cool place for at least 24 hours. Meantime chop the goose fat quite small and put it with ½ pint of water to melt slowly.

When they are ready, brush the salt from the pieces of goose and immerse them in the pan of fat. Should there not be enough to cover all, add melted pork fat. Cook slowly for 2½ hours or until the meat is easily pierced by a skewer (in the south-west of France they use a straw to test), which must pierce easily and completely. Take the pieces of goose from the fat and drain them well; then stow them in deep earthenware crocks (very difficult to find nowadays) or pack them in cocottes. Decant the fat and heat it until it ceases to splutter, allow it to cool slightly then pour it over the goose packed in the cocottes and clear away into a cool larder. When the pots are quite cold, seal the top surface with good parchment paper cut to size; and your confit will keep for the best part of a year.

So much then for the first part of the preparation of a cassoulet, though confit has several other preparations in its own right.

165 Confit d'Oie aux Pommes de Terre

Cut some potatoes into fingers as for fried potatoes (wrongly known as chips). Give them their first fry, drain them, change them into a thick frying-pan, add the required pieces of confit and sauté to finish the cooking. Season with salt and pepper then add a clove of garlic chopped finely with parsley. Having drained the fat from the poêle, sauter so as to mix all well together.

166 Confit d'Oie aux Petits Pois

Take the required number of pieces of confit from the goose fat and put them in a warm place to drain. Meantime put 12 small onions and 4 oz. ham cut into small dice, together with a spoonful of the goose fat, into a thick-bottomed pan. When these have taken on a slight brownish colour, add a quart of young peas and a bouquet garni; then put on a tight-fitting lid and continue the cooking at a reduced heat. Shake the pan from time to time and take care that the peas do not brown. After 15 minutes put a glass of water into the pan and allow the cooking to continue without the lid. Remove the bouquet garni, add a spoonful of sugar and the peas are ready for use. Now put in the pieces of confit to heat and to serve place the peas in the bottom of the dish with the confit of goose on top.

There you have two ways of dealing with the remains of the bird which furnishes foie gras. They are dishes as served by the peasant farmers in S.W. France to entertain the unexpected guest. A salad and cheese to follow with rough wine to drink —one can ask nothing better.

167 Cassoulet

There are three ways of making a cassoulet and variations of each of these. Toulouse, Carcassonne and Castelnaudary each have their methods and differing ingredients. These include a selection from Confit d'Oie, chunks cut from a leg of mutton or even half a small leg of the same, pork chops, pickled pork, saucission à l'ail, couennes de porc (fresh pork skin), perhaps an old partridge and pork sausages (blanched, skinned and cut into ¼-in. slices). The most important ingredient is, of course, the haricots blancs. These should have been soaked in cold water overnight and put on to cook next morning in a change of water, with garlic, onion and a bouquet garni.

When the white haricots are half cooked begin the building up of the cassoulet. Line the interior of one of the special squat glazed earthenware dishes with pieces of couennes, with a layer of beans over, and continue to build up with pieces of confit, slices of saucisson, pork and/or mutton, not forgetting the garlic. Cover with more of the beans and a sprinkling of bread raspings. Put a ladleful of the bean cooking liquor over, place on the lid and push into a moderate oven. There are some who thicken this liquor slightly, others add a skinned, de-seeded ripe tomato or a spoonful of tomato purée. Again, others withdraw the dishes from the oven several times, push the browning raspings down into the liquid and re-sprinkle. The dish must go to the table brown on top.

168 Civet de Venaison

This dish is similar in preparation to Sauté de Boeuf with the important exception that the name Civet is reserved for furred game (hare or venison), and that the sauce is bound with the blood of the animal. This is added at the end of the cooking period, as the civet must not then boil again.

The procedure is the same. The meat from the leg is cut into convenient-sized pieces. Add one-quarter of its bulk in pickled flank of pork in pieces of the same size. The meat is first sautéd in oil and then put on to cook in half red wine, half venison stock. The garnish is button mushrooms, small onions and croûtons of fried bread.

169 Civet de Venaison aux Marrons

As above, substituting twice the amount of peeled chestnuts for the mushrooms. The chestnuts are finished along with the meat in the sauce.

170 Pigeonneaux aux Petits Pois

Truss young pigeons and brown them slightly in butter. Then arrange them in casseroles with ½ pint of shelled green peas, 8 or 10 button onions and a spoonful of blanched and fried dice of pickled belly pork for every 2 birds. Allow these to cook together very gently with a bouquet garni in the midst and a little reduced chicken stock over.

171 Pigeon en Compote

As in the above method the pigeon, after being coloured in butter, is put to cook in a casserole. This time with a garnish of turned olives, lardoons of blanched belly pork, button onions and button mushrooms.

172 Salmis of Wood Pigeon

If you live in the country, no doubt these farmers' pests will have been offered to you many times. They are good eating, and useful to you as a cook in your search for variety in your menu. Braise them in the oven on a bed of vegetables with the giblets and a little stock. They will be of all ages so remove them as and when they are cooked.

Divide each bird into two and take away breastbone, backbone and skin. Now make a fine farce from sausage-meat by adding Duxelles together with a little finely chopped fines herbes. Put a pad of this under the leg of each half bird and another on the inside. This will cook sufficiently during the preliminary heating prior to service.

For the sauce, put the hearts, gizzards and some of the braising vegetables through the liquidizer and thin this purée to a workable consistency with some of the stock and a little brown sauce to bind. Rectify the seasoning. Dress the half birds on shaped bread croûtons fried in butter and sauce over with the sauce salmi. Braised celery is a suitable accompanying vegetable.

173 Braised Saddle of Hare

The saddle should be larded with strips of larding bacon inserted in neat rows before marinading or, if time is lacking, wrapped in a thin sheet of larding bacon, which is secured with string. Use the marinading vegetables as a bed under the saddle during the braising. Serve with a Sauce Poivrade and, as with all dishes of hare, Red Currant Jelly.

174 Jugged Hare (Civet de Lièvre)

The Scottish Mountain (white) Hare is suitable for this dish; it is not so large as the brown hare, is cheaper and quite as good from a culinary point of view. Skin and eviscerate the animal, collecting the blood and removing carefully the gall-bag from the liver.

I strongly advise your taking the fillets from the back, starting at the shoulder through to the back legs. Sections of these beaten out fairly thin will give escalopes which may form the basis of many entrées. Do not forget that there is a 'filet mignon' under the backbone. Use the legs only for the civet; shortening the fore-legs at the 'elbow' and boning out the hind legs, each of which you cut into two. Do not chop these; hare leg bones splinter into sharp fragments which can be dangerous.

Sauté these pieces of leg in oil with 8 oz. per hare of blanched lean belly pork cut into cubes, 2 or 3 onions cut into eighths, and a sprinkling of flour. Next change the pieces into another casserole, soak off any glaze there may be on the sautoir with an inexpensive wine (or the collected remnants of decanted bottles, themselves decanted) and add sufficient stock made from the carcasses of the hares to cover the civet. Place a bouquet garni, enclosing 2 crushed cloves of garlic, in the centre and cook gently on a corner of the stove. When this is accomplished, strain off the cooking liquor and thicken it with the heart, lungs, liver and kidneys, plus the collected blood, which you have passed through the liquidizer. Replace the pieces of hare in this sauce, which you must not boil. Then add the garnish, which consists of button onions (cooked with butter, pinch of sugar and seasoning) and button mushrooms cooked in stock, failing these use small mushrooms cut into four.

In the old days some French cooks used to escalope the hare liver, sauté it and add to the dished-up hare; but you will perhaps agree that the puréed liver makes a finer sauce.

175 Râble de Lièvre

This comprises the whole of the back of the hare from the neck to the haunches; but I advise you to shorten this to the same proportions as a saddle of mutton and remove the tendons.

176 Râble de Lièvre à la Crème

Marinade the back or backs of hare in a marinade of sliced carrots, onions, celery, 2 cloves of garlic, parsley roots, a branch of thyme, 2 cloves, a few broken peppercorns and a crumbled bayleaf, mixed with white wine and half the amount in wine vinegar together with a few spoonfuls of oil. Having mixed the backs of hare in this marinade keep them in an earthenware crock for a few days in a cool place in the larder.

Cook the râble on a bed of the marinading vegetables in a hot oven and when it is nearly cooked remove these and pour over it thick cream and continue basting with this. Serve the râble with the strained cream to which you have added a squeeze of lemon juice.

177 Raised Grouse Pie

Use a 5½-in. diameter pie mould, 4 in. deep (the type that is hinged and fastened with a skewer). You will require 1½ lb. of either short or pie paste. The crust is not important, for most people leave it on the plate. Roll this paste into a ball and pin it out into a round sheet, but not too thin. Flour the top surface well and fold it into two by bringing the far edge towards you. This will give a half-moon shape with a double thickness in front of you. Endeavour by compressing it gently to bring this curve into a more or less straight line and give it a roll away from you, making a bag shape; but take care not to burst the bag if you have trapped any air inside it. Place the pie mould on a baking sheet as it does not have a bottom and proceed to insert the bag. Ease out the paste with your fingers and press well into any decorations there may be on the tin mould, taking great care not to break or crack the dough. The whole object of this operation is to have a seamless lining so that you will not have the vexatious sight of an ugly crack or opening seam, allowing all the essential goodness you have introduced into the pie to drain away during baking. Trim away the surplus paste at the top, leaving a standing edge of about ½ in. above the top of the mould.

Next line the interior with streaky bacon. Tear off feathers and skin from 4 old grouse, and put the breasts minus tendons to soak in a glass of whisky. Take the meat from the thighs and chop it finely with the livers and a small onion. Mix this mince with 1¾ lb. of pork sausage-meat to make a farce. Plaster a thin layer of this over the lining of streaky bacon. Now proceed to fill the mould, using alternate layers of grouse fillets and farce, incorporating any dribbles of whisky there may be left. Make the last layer one of farce.

Endeavour to give the top a dome. Roof this over with a sheet of paste made from the assembled trimmings. Then, having sealed this to the wall of the pie with a pinched border, use up any left-over bits of pastry as leaves, roses or other ornamentations you may fancy. Wash this over with a yolk of egg beaten with a little milk, allow to lie for an hour and bake in a moderate oven for 2 hours. Meantime prepare a stock from the carcasses and giblets.

You should reduce this well, and, to make sure that it will set firmly, add 1½ oz. gelatine to a pint.

When the pie is baked, remove the tin mould and varnish the sides with the egg/milk wash and return the pie to the oven for a minute to set this. Allow both pie and gravy to cool, but not get cold, before filling with the latter.

VEAL, HAM

178 Blanquette de Veau à l'Ancienne

Cut, as for a stew, sufficient pieces of veal from breast and shoulder and put them on to cook with an onion stuck with a clove, 2 carrots, a bouquet garni and a branch of celery. Cover this barely with white veal stock and season. Bring to the boil, remove the scum, reduce the heat and continue cooking slowly under a cover. Meantime, peel button onions and put them on to cook in veal stock with a pat of butter and seasoning. Likewise trim the stalks of button mushrooms, or if they are overgrown turn them, and put them on to cook in stock.

When they are ready, strain the stock from these three elements and reduce it, meanwhile keeping the veal, onions and mushrooms under cover in the bain marie. Thicken the stock with a roux of butter and flour and continue to reduce, then finally bind the sauce with a liaison of yolks, cream and the juice of half a lemon. Mix this sauce with the veal, onions and mushrooms, and the blanquette is ready to serve. When the blanquette is dressed, garnish the dish with fried bread croûtons in the shape of leaves.

179 Ris de Veau

Sweetbreads need preliminary treatment. Soak them in running water for several hours to get rid of as much blood as possible. Blanch them, refresh them under the cold tap; and, when they are cool, proceed to remove as much as you can of the fibres and cartilages by passing your fingers between the folds of the sweetbreads. When this is done put a clean kitchen cloth on a baking sheet and arrange the sweetbreads on it, cover with rest of the cloth or another one, put another baking sheet on top; and add a weight to press.

Next day the sweetbreads should be larded with strips of larding bacon in neat rows. Then put them on to braise under cover, on a bed of sliced onions and carrots, with a good brown stock.

Braising is not the only method of dealing with sweetbreads. After the initial treatment, they may be grilled either whole, split lengthwise or in escalopes. In escalopes they can be passed through melted butter and fine breadcrumbs, then sauté. Or, in escalopes again, they can be seasoned, floured and sauté in butter.

Sweetbreads come to you in pairs. One is a plump oval in shape and is known as the heart sweetbread; the other, the throat is irregular in shape and terminates in two long fingers. This is best used for brouchées, as a filling for croustades, or in crêpinettes.

180 Crêpinettes de Ris de Veau

Take some pig's caul and soak it in cold water so that it will stretch. Cut sweetbread trimmings, end pieces or misshapen throat breads into dice. Add to these half the amount, in dice, of cooked belly pork. If you can spare a few truffles cut them also into dice, saving one round slice to go under the crêpine on top of the farce in each crêpinette. Mix with a quarter of the weight of the breads in farce fine de porc, or failing that sausage-meat, and add a raw egg to the mixture.

Spread squares of the crêpine out on the table; and on each put an amount of the above mixture the size of a large egg (say about 3 oz.) and spread this in a rectangular shape. Fold over the crêpine to make little packets, remembering the truffle slices if you have them. Coat the top with melted butter and sprinkle with breadcrumbs. For service, cook these crêpinettes in the oven for a few minutes, then give the crumbs a golden tinge under the griller. Serve with Sauce Madère.

181 Jamon* Jerez

For this, heat boiled ham in a pale sherry to which you have added a little water and see that it does not boil. Lift out the ham and withdraw the pan from the heat. Add a few pats of fresh butter to the liquid and whisk vigorously between additions. The heat must not be more than will soften the butter; if this is oiled the sherry will not amalgamate. Use this sherry/butter sauce over the ham and garnish with new peas.

182 Jambon* braisé aux Epinards

Cut the requisite amount of boiled ham and warm it in hot water to which you have added a spoonful of Sauce Madére. Use a shallow pan and take care that the liquid does not boil.

Use spinach beet for the garnish; a row or two sown in spring will furnish your requirements during the season. The leaves are larger than those of true spinach and the mid rubs more robust, both of which make for a saving of time stripping. Wash well to eliminate grit, etc., and cook in boiling salted water. Refresh with cold water, then lift out the spinach with your hands to drain (avoiding the last remnants of grit) and squeeze out most of the surplus moisture. Chop roughly and re-heat in butter, seasoning with pepper, salt and a pinch of grated nutmeg.

To serve, put the spinach in a neatly moulded pile at one side of the dish, arrange the slices of ham alongside, add a touch of Madeira to the sauce before using it to cover the ham.

* 'Jamon' in Spanish = 'Jambon' in French.

We hear much from those writers on cookery matters, who themselves are not cooks, concerning the re-heating of cooked meats. I agree with all they say about the warming-up of roast meats; nothing can replace a cut from a freshly roasted joint —a warmed up slice of meat from yesterday's sirloin is an abomination—BUT, and I stake a sixty years' reputation here, there is no reason why a boiled ham—or a boiled joint—should not be reheated.

183 Saucisses à la mode d'Alsace

This very simple but worthwhile dish is easily prepared. Use round cocottes that have lids and put in the bottom 1½-in. layer of peeled, cored and sliced Bramley Seedling or other cooking apples that fall into a purée on cooking. On this layer place 6 uncooked pork sausages; it does not matter if you have to squeeze them in for they will shrink slightly on cooking. Place another similar layer of sliced apples over, put on the lid and into the oven. They do not take long to cook, and can be kept in the hot cupboard and sent to the table in the cocottes as they are.

VEGETABLES

184 Asperges

Undo the bundles and immerse the asparagus in cold water. Then remove those bracts or immature leaves which occur on the stalks under the growing head. Afterwards scrape the hard white root end of the stems and assemble the asparagus in bundles of ten or twelve with the heads level and tie the root ends with string. Cut this end level then carefully draw the heads together and secure them with raffia. Put the bundles to cook in salted water at the boil, but keep them at simmering point. They will take about 20 minutes. Cool them under running water. To serve, reheat in hot water, drain well, then dress on a folded serviette accompanied by a sauce-boat of melted butter or Hollandaise sauce.

185 Aubergines farcies à l'Egyptienne

Cut the aubergines in two lengthwise, run a knife around the edge without cutting the skin and make a few criss-cross cuts in the pulp. Fry the aubergines gently in olive oil, cut side down, so that the interior may be removed. Chop this and mix with chopped onion allowed to fall in oil, with a little garlic added. Season and refill the aubergine skins, place on top of them a row of sliced tomatoes and arrange them in oven dishes. On withdrawing them from the oven sprinkle a little chopped parsley over.

186 Imam Bayeldi (*Aubergines*)

Take the required number of aubergines and, according to their girth, make three or four cuts in them nearly the whole length; but do not cut through the bottom skin. Place them in the oven until they begin to wilt. Meantime prepare a little stew of chopped onions, garlic and blanched and de-seeded tomatoes cooked in oil. Season with salt, pepper and a pinch of sugar. Allow to cool a little, then stuff the incisions you have made in the aubergines with this mixture. Sprinkle with oil, then breadcrumbs, and put into the oven until they are cooked through. Dust with chopped parsley before serving. Aubergines cooked in this way are excellent when cold.

187 Artichauts

Trim the base of each, taking care to rub any exposed part with a cut lemon, and shorten the leaves by one-third. If the artichokes are very large, it will be necessary to tie them with string to prevent the loss of leaves during the cooking. Boil them in salted water, refresh under the cold water and remove the 'chokes'. Keep them upside down on an earthenware dish in the larder. If they are to be served cold, dress them on a papered dish and send a Sauce Vinaigrette with them. If hot, they must be re-heated in salted water, drained, dressed on a folded serviette and served with either melted butter, Sauce Mousseline or Sauce Hollandaise.

188 Betteraves à la Bordelaise

Cut thick rounds of cooked beetroot, and to ensure that they are all of the same size pass a crimped cutter over them, then hollow out the tops with a round vegetable scoop. Chop an onion mixed with a touch of garlic and fry slightly in oil, add some decanted remains of Bordeaux wine and boil until the onions are quite cooked. Next add a spoonful or two of thick brown sauce and continue boiling until this stuffing has a good consistency. Fill the hollowed out beetroot shapes and keep them, with a piece of greased paper over, in the hot cupboard until wanted for service. A fleck of chopped parsley on top before sending to the table is an improvement.

189 Choux Farcis

Take the leaves from a young cabbage, remove the mid-ribs and blanch the tender green leafy parts. Take as much pork sausage-meat as will give a ball the size of a walnut for each cabbage, add a handful or so of freshly-made white breadcrumbs and enough of the finely grated mid-ribs to give a workable consistency. Mix well together. Now take 3 or 4 of the young leaves and place a ball of this stuffiing in the middle. Fold over the leaves and form into a ball in a clean kitchen cloth by squeezing and twisting. Place these little stuffed cabbages on an oven dish furnished with a lid, put a ladleful or two of stock in the bottom, cover and place in the oven until they are cooked.

190 Choux-fleurs Dubarry

Cook the florets of cauliflower in salted water. Refresh them, drain and mould in semi-spherical moulds or failing these in suitable basins. Unmould on to fireproof dishes, sauce with a light Béchamel sauce (in which a little of the cooking liquor has been incorporated), sprinkle with grated cheese and gratinate when required.

191 Choux-fleurs Beurre Noisette

Deal with the cauliflowers as above as far as the cooking and moulding is concerned. Then, at the moment of service, sprinkle them with lemon juice and throw over them a beurre noisette in which you have browned a few dried breadcrumbs.

192 Choux-fleurs Polonaise

This is a slightly more elaborate dressing then the last. Push some hard-boiled eggs through the sieve and sprinkle these over the moulded cauliflowers with the addition of a little chopped parsley before the lemon juice, the beurre noisette and browned breadcrumbs.

193 Carottes Vichy

Slice the scraped carrots on the mandoline and put them on to cook with sufficient water for them to bathe freely. Season with salt, pepper and sugar, with a pat of butter. Then boil, first under cover, then until almost complete evaporation of the liquid. Sprinkle with chopped parsley.

194 Carrots, Turnips, Button Onions for garnish

The carrots and turnips are cut into the shape of elongated barrels 2 in. long with six sides—the small onions are just peeled and if necessary reduced in size. Keep the three elements separate. They are all cooked in water with salt, pepper and a little sugar, with a pat of butter. Start them off under cover, then remove the lid and reduce the liquor by fast boiling to a glaze.

195 Céleris Braisé

Remove the outside stalks, shorten those that are left and trim the root end. Give the celery a wash under the running cold water and put on to blanch. After cooling them take each one and holding the now more pliable stalks slightly apart, direct a powerful stream of cold water to dislodge every particle of grit which may be lodged where stalk meets root. If there is any suspicion of stringiness in the outside of the exposed stalks, remove the filaments with a potato knife. Next put the celery on to braise in salted water with a covering of beef kidney fat or, failing that, with strained fat skimmed from the stock-pot.

When the celery is cooked and cold remove the fat, cut each head into two lengthwise, fold in half and trim. Arrange on shallow trays with some of the cooking liquor and a sheet of paper over. Warm through on the hot-plate. Sauce according to the entrée.

196 Concombre Farci

Peel a cucumber and cut it across into 2-in. sections. Take out a ball of the seedy inside with a round vegetable scoop, and fill the space it occupied with Duxelles (page ooo) with which you have mixed half its weight in pork sausage-meat. Give the top a rounded surface, sprinkle it with fresh breadcrumbs and cook in the oven under cover of a buttered paper. At the moment of service heat the stuffed cucumbers in a shallow tray with a little water in the bottom and a paper over, then brown the breadcrumbs slightly.

197 Fèves au Lard

Shell broad beans, boil them in salted water and having cooled them remove the skins. Next make a little sauce by cooking slowly without browning a handful of lardons (cut from cooked salt flank of pork) in a little pork fat. Add to this an onion chopped but not too small. Stir in a teaspoonful or so of flour and use the liquor in which the beans were cooked to make the sauce. Into this you mix the skinned beans. Season carefully and add chopped savory to flavour.

198 Haricots Bretonne

Soak the white haricots overnight. Next day change the water and put them on to cook with a carrot cut into four, an onion with 2 cloves stuck in it, a small handful of salt and a bouquet garni. Meantime prepare a *Sauce Bretonne* by chopping an onion finely and allowing it to fall in pork fat. Complete the cooking by adding 2 small ladles of tomato sauce and 2 of brown, a suspicion of garlic is also indicated here. Use this sauce to bind the drained haricots and sprinkle with chopped parsley when serving.

199 Poireaux Braisés

Wash a bunch of leeks, remove the outer leaf, trim the roots and cut off the green parts. Tie the whites into bundles and boil them in salted water. They may now be treated as a vegetable and be served with melted butter, Sauce Hollandaise or Mousseline. Alternatively they can be cut into 1½-in. lengths, drained, dipped in frying batter and fried in hot fat.

200 Vegetable Marrow

If you grow them and can bring yourself to use them when they are about 6 in. long, cut off flower and stalk ends, then divide into three. Push the interior down and stuff with a light stuffing of chopped cooked onion, cooked meat and breadcrumbs bound with a little tomato sauce. Bake them on a greased plaque in the oven with a paper cover. Serve with an appropriate sauce or gratinate.

201 Courge au Beurre

When the vegetable marrows are bigger, peel them and cut them across into 3-in. sections. Take out the seeds, cut the sections into convenient pieces, and trim the corners. Put these on to cook in butter under cover. This method is preferable to boiling.

202 Piments Doux or Poivrons

Pack the peppers tightly in an earthenware casserole furnished with a lid. Even though you crack them in doing so, it is of no consequence as they shrink very much on cooking. Pour over them some olive oil, season, then on with the lid and into the oven. They are useful as an hors d'oeuvre, as a garnish or vegetable.

Green peppers as above may also be stuffed with pilaff rice mixed with diced ham and mushrooms.

203 Petits Pois à la Française

Put a quart of shelled young, green peas into a casserole with a glass of water, a piece of butter the size of a hen's egg, a teaspoonful of sugar, 12 spring onions, salt and pepper. Cover with a tightly-fitting lid and cook on a moderate heat, shaking the pan occasionally. When they are about cooked, mix a spoonful of flour into another good pat of butter and put this *beurre manié* into the pan with the peas. Shake about to thicken any liquid there may be left.

In most French cookery books where the preparation of Petits Pois à la Française is being discussed, one is instructed to put a layer of shredded lettuce at the bottom of the pan. This cannot serve any useful purpose and has one grave disadvantage; it may incommode a guest, for no one would wish to see a guest with a long strip of cooked lettuce hanging, like a piece of string, from the corner of his mouth.

204 Pommes Anna

Choose long potatoes and cut them into cylinders or push a column cutter over them. Then slice them on the mandoline into discs the size of a two-shilling-piece. Wash these in cold water and dry them on a clean cloth. If you do not have a Pomme Anna mould, a small sauteuse, pancake pan or small omelette pan will do. Butter the bottom of the mould or pan and begin putting the slices of potato in overlapping concentric circles. Season each layer with a little fine salt and run a small amount of clarified butter over. Continue thus for six layers. Place a lid on the pan and put it in the oven. When the potatoes are cooked, drain off the butter, then reverse the pan on to the service dish.

Some potatoes seem to stick to the mould more readily than others so I offer you this tip. Put a circle of cartridge paper (i.e. the paper used by artists in water colours) in the bottom of the pan used for Pommes Anna and proceed as above. Provided that the sides of the pan are free, you will not have any difficulty in turning out the potatoes and the paper should come off very easily. It is a good plan to unmould Pommes Anna on to an upturned lid. This enables you to drain off the butter and then to slide the potatoes on to the service dish.

205 Pommes Allumettes

A smaller cut of potato than ordinary fried ones, say about $\frac{3}{16}$-in.-square section. Slightly bigger than straw potatoes.

206 Pommes Alphonse

Scrub the potatoes, peel one strip all the way round and steam them. This enables you to lift off easily the remaining two pieces of skin when cooked. Next slice them in thick slices, bind them with Beurre Maître d'Hotel, season, sprinkle them with grated cheese and gratinate.

207 Pommes Ambassadeur

This dish is sometimes known as *Pommes Voisin*. When making Pommes Anna sprinkle the layers with grated cheese, and deal with them in the same way.

208 Pommes au Four

These are scrubbed potatoes baked in the oven. On removing them a refinement is to burst them by squeezing and insert a pat of butter.

209 Pommes Nature

Put them on to boil in cold water with a handful of salt, and cook slowly for about 30 minutes. Test them with a skewer and if they are cooked drain off the water (which may be useful in a pulse soup). Then cover them with a clean kitchen cloth, put on the lid and keep hot on the hot-plate.

210 Pommes Boulangère

Peel the required amount of potatoes and slice them on the mandoline. Next peel one-quarter of this amount in onions and slice them also. Mix the two together with a seasoning of pepper and salt. Then mix in a ladle or two of the fat rendered by a roast joint of mutton and a little stock. Cover with a sheet of grease-proof paper and cook in the oven. At one time it was the practice to roast a leg of mutton with a bed of Pommes Boulangère below it.

211 Pommes à la Crème

For this choose non-floury potatoes, scrub them and cook them in salted water. Peel them and cut into fairly thick slices, then put them with hot milk to boil, seasoning with salt, pepper and a trace of grated nutmeg. Reduce the mixture by rapid boiling, stirring the while: it will probably be found that some thickening takes place. Add some fresh cream to finish and stir it in, taking care not to break the slices unduly.

212 Pommes Château

Cut some large potatoes across in slices 1¾-in. thick; and then cut these slices again into pieces which will enable you to pare them down to a barrel shape, with six sides and two flat ends. Blanch them and cool under the cold water tap. Have ready an oven plaque or a roasting tin with some hot fat. Then, when you have drained the potatoes, put them into the fat, turn them about and put them into the oven to cook.

When ready they should be drained of the fat and kept warm in the hot-plate; so that when they are required for service you can sauté them for a few minutes in butter.

213 Pommes Duchesse

Put on to cook in the usual way the required amount of peeled potatoes, each cut into four. Then drain and dry them for a few minutes on the stove. Next put them through the sieve or the potato ricer, bind them with a few yolks of eggs, verify the seasoning and add a little grated nutmeg. The mixture should then be piped in rosettes on to a buttered plaque, from a bag and star tube. When required for service put these into a hot oven to brown the top surface slightly.

The Pommes Duchesse mixture may be allowed to cool and then be moulded by hand into fancy shapes, brioches, petits pains, little cakes, etc., which can be egg-washed and browned quickly in a hot oven; but this is a time-wasting operation.

214 Pommes Chip

These are potatoes cut into thin discs about the size of a half-crown, which are fried crisp in deep fat and usually served with roast game. They are somewhat similar to what we know as Potato Crisps.

What are known this side of the Channel as chips are *Pommes Frites* or *Pommes Pont-Neuf*.

215 Pommes Hongroise

Chop an onion finely and allow it to fall without browning in pork fat, then add ½ a dessertspoonful of Paprika pepper and stir in well. Then put about 2 lb. turned potatoes with sufficient fond blanc barely to cover them. Cook until the liquid is reduced to a sauce and season with salt. Some cooks add chopped tomato flesh to the mixture, but this is not essential. The main thing is to have the potatoes almost the colour of a goulash.

216 Hashed Brown Potatoes

This is a manner of cooking potatoes which is popular with Americans. Cook the required amount of potatoes, boiling or steaming them in their skins. Have ready a frying-pan with some hot rendered pork fat, in which you have lightly fried a small quantity of chopped onion. Peel the cooked potatoes, put them in the hot fat and crush them with the back of a fork. Toss them occasionally allowing time for the potatoes to take colour between each tossing. Season with pepper and salt and fold over or make them into small cakes which should have another fry on each side.

I am quite aware that in America onion is not usually added to this dish, but I think you will agree with me that its addition is an improvement.

217 Pommes Nouvelles

These are best washed carefully to remove the soil or sand; but if the potatoes are really new they should not be scrubbed hard enough to remove the skin. Boil them in salted water with a sprig of fresh mint, or steam them with a branch of mint laid over them. To serve, roll them in fresh butter or place a pat of fresh butter on top.

218 Pommes à la Lyonnaise

Cut some cold boiled potatoes into not too thin slices and sauté them in oil. Next sauté in oil some sliced onions (cutting the outer rings in four). Drain the two and finish them in butter together. Use roughly quarter the amount of potatoes in fried onions. Be sure to sauté well together, so that you mix them thoroughly, and season.

219 Pommes à la Parisienne

Cut little balls from a variety of large potatoes, using a vegetable scoop about $\frac{3}{4}$ in. in diameter. Blanch them and cook in butter until they are nicely browned, roll them in melted glace de viande before serving.

220 Pommes Parmentier

The potatoes are cut into cubes about $\frac{5}{8}$-in. sides, blanched, cooled and cooked in butter. Sprinkle with chopped parsley when serving.

221 Purée de Pommes de Terre

Cut peeled potatoes into quarters and put them on to boil with salted water. As soon as they are cooked, either squeeze them through the ricer or push them through a sieve. Mix butter with them at the rate of say 3 or 4 oz. to every 2 lb.; and finally add $\frac{1}{3}$ of a pint of *boiling* milk.

Mashed potatoes do not keep very well on the hot-plate, they tend to stiffen up and lose all their qualities. If therefore you have a busy lunch service and wish to earn and keep a reputation for your excellent Purée de Pommes de Terre, cook them in relays.

222 Roast Potatoes

Cut the potatoes into two or four according to size and thereafter treat them as explained under Pommes de Terre Château.

223 Pommes Soufflées

Trim some peeled potatoes to give you either rectangles or ovals when sliced, and cut them into even slices $\frac{1}{8}$ in. to $\frac{3}{16}$ in. in

top left:
Cotelettes froides en macédoine

top right:
Imam Bayeldi

centre:
Stuffed cucumbers

bottom left:
Stuffed tomatoes

bottom right:
Tournedos Choron

thickness. Dry on a cloth. Have ready two pans of deep fat (or better, oil), one moderately hot and the other very hot. Put a frying basket into the moderately hot fat and throw in a few of the sliced potatoes singly, if you throw them by the handful they may remain in one lump of wasted effort. The object of this is to cook the slices without browning them. Verify the state of cooking by pinching a slice between thumb and forefinger. If you are satisfied that the slices are cooked, remove them from the fat. Then when they are required for service plunge them into the hot fat; they should souffler at once.

It is as well to make a few trials of different potatoes before attempting the main fry.

224 Pommes Croquettes

Take the required amount of the Pommes Duchesse mixture and shape into desired forms on a floured table; cork shapes are most practical. Pass them through beaten, seasoned egg, then breadcrumbs and fry in the deep fat.

Many shapes may be tried but I advise you to stick to those that are not likely to come adrift during the frying. In addition to the cork shapes mentioned above there are balls (about 1¼ in. in diameter), pear shapes of similar size, little cakes (2 in. in diameter and ½ in. thick) rectangles or fingers, or shapes cut out with a crimped cutter from a sheet of Pommes Duchesse. All must be egg and breadcrumbed.

225 Pommes Saint-Florentin

Use the Duchesse mixture and incorporate one-eighth of its volume in small dice of lean cooked ham. Roll this out and cut off into pieces about the size of a cork. Pass them through beaten egg and Vermicelle crushed small, and then flatten them slightly with the flat of a knife giving them a rectangular shape. Fry them in the deep fat.

226 Pommes Marquise

Reduce some tomato purée of a good colour to a paste and use enough of it to tint some Pommes Duchesse. From a bag and star tube, pipe the potato on to greased sheet tins in the shape of half-meringue shells. Wash the tops carefully with beaten egg and place in a hot oven for a minute prior to service.

227 Soufflé aux Epinards

Take about 8 oz. washed spinach, cook it in salted water in the ordinary way, drain it well and pass it through the sieve. Bind it with 3 yolks, add a small handful of grated Parmesan cheese and then mix in carefully 4 whites beaten stiffly. Fill either a well-buttered soufflé mould or several buttered dariole moulds. These latter need not be filled to the top as they are apt to become top-heavy when unmoulded. Cook in a water bath in the oven with a sheet of greased paper over.

228 Stuffed Tomatoes

Stand each tomato on the stalk end and cut across about one-quarter of the way down from the flower end. Empty the seeds and liquid from the inside, either by using a round vegetable scoop, or if you have only a few to do, by means of the handle of a coffee-spoon. (This latter is preferable as only the seeds and water are removed, and the segmental walls are undisturbed. Of course if you have a number to do, the vegetable scoop is quicker.) I maintain that a stuffed tomato stands better and rocks about less if stood on the stalk end than on the flower end. It used to be the practice, when tomatoes were more or less oval or irregular in shape, to cut them in two lengthwise and empty by squeezing out the seeds and water; but with modern tomatoes smaller and round in shape one risks unnecessarily the breaking of the flesh.

(*a*) Stuff the tomato shells with Duxelles, making a dome on top, and sprinkle with breadcrumbs. Place the stuffed tomatoes on a greased or oiled oven plaque and put them in the oven with a sheet of paper on top. They do not take long to cook; so beware of over-cooking, for if this happens they will collapse and be useless.

(*b*) Tomatoes may be stuffed with scrambled eggs with or without an admixture of small dice of cooked York ham. The caps may be replaced or the filling sprinkled with grated Parmesan cheese. In the latter case, after cooking in the oven as above, gratinate slightly under the salamander.

(*c*) As above, this time use sliced hard-boiled eggs which are cut into dice then bound with a creamy Sauce Béchamel as a filling. Sprinkle with grated cheese and put the tray of tomatoes into the oven, removing them when they are cooked. If necessary, a moment or two under the salamander will gratinate them.

(*d*) Cooked chicken may be cut into neat cubes or chopped, bound with a Suprême or other suitable sauce and used as a filling for the hollowed-out tomatoes. After cooking these may be gratinated or not as desired.

(*e*) Soak fine white breadcrumbs in milk or consommé and squeeze out the surplus moisture. Add twice the volume in chopped cooked (left-over) meat; ham, poultry, beef from the pot-au-feu or lamb. Sauter in butter an appropriate quantity of finely chopped onion with a touch of garlic. Add this to the mixture together with chopped herbs (tarragon, chervil, parsley) and bind with beaten raw egg. Fill into the tomato shells and put a knob of butter on each before baking in the oven.

(*f*) Prepare a Risotto alla Piemontese and use this to fill the tomatoes. Place a tiny knob of butter on each tomato, cook and gratinate at the same time in a hot oven.

(*g*) Use well-shaped round tomatoes, remove the stalks and cut them into halves at the 'equator' by making V-shaped cuts to the centre with a pointed sharp knife. Separate the halves and empty seeds and water, then with a vegetable scoop take out some of the core. Make the stuffing from sausage-meat slackened with tomato purée and seasoned with chopped fines herbes and cooked chopped shallot. Season the halves of tomato and pipe this stuffing over them from a bag and tube. Then bake in the oven.

229 Tomates à la Hussarde (1)

Make a little stew by cutting into dice, poivrons, mushrooms, gherkins and either cooked ham or tongue, then tossing them in butter until the first two have fallen. Bind with a well-reduced Béchamel Sauce and use to fill tomatoes emptied of seeds and water. Put them on an oven dish and into the oven until the tomatoes are just cooked and no more.

230 Tomates à la Hussarde (2)

Cut the tomatoes one-quarter of the way down from the flower end as already instructed and, having removed the stalk, stand them on an oven dish and remove the core, seeds and water. Chop sufficient onions with a touch of garlic and cook them gently in oil. Mix with these a little chopped parsley, ham and mushroom. Season liberally with paprika, add white breadcrumbs to make a crumbly consistency and use to fill the tomatoes. Anoint with a few drops of oil and cook in the oven.

231 Tomates à l'Avignonnaise

Take the required number of aubergines. See that they are young. Peel them and cut each into three lengthwise. This will give you three slices about ½ in. in thickness. Fry these on both sides in oil and arrange them on earthenware oven dishes. Peel and drain (of seeds and water) sufficient tomatoes; chop them roughly and cook them gently in oil with a little finely chopped onion and the essential garlic. Season and mix with them sufficient fresh breadcrumbs to mop up all the liquid and pile this over the aubergine slices. Sprinkle bread raspings over (or crushed bread crusts which have been dried in the oven), and allow them to stew gently in a cool oven until ready for service.

SWEETS & PASTRY

VARIOUS FRUIT DISHES

232 Baked Apple

Push an apple corer through the apples and cut off the blossom end to act as a plug at the stalk end. Place this in position and fill the interior with brown sugar or mincemeat, marmalade or sultanas. With a sharp knife make a cut around the 'equator' so that the skin will be free to lift during the cooking. Baked apples are best cooked in a roasting tin with a cover and about ½ in. of water in the bottom of the tin. Serve with whipped cream in a sauce-boat, or pipe it on the apples if cold.

233 Blackcurrant Shortcake

Make into a short paste: ¾ lb. flour, ½ lb. butter, ¼ lb. caster sugar, 1 teaspoonful of bicarbonate of soda and ¼ teaspoonful of ground cinnamon.

These quantities make 7 rounds of shortcake so one must be halved when sandwiching together. Put a circle of greaseproof paper in the bottom of seven 6-in. sandwich pans and divide the above dough between them. Press this out evenly because it is too short to roll. Then bake in a moderate oven as for shortbread.

When baked and cool, remove the papers and sandwich with black currants stewed with sugar to the consistency of jam. It is better to thicken the syrup slightly with arrowroot rather than reduce it by boiling as this tends to toughen the black currants. A knife with a saw edge must be used to cut the shortcakes into four with a sawing motion, as they are very fragile. Serve with a blob of whipped cream on top of the sugar-dusted portions.

234 Raspberry or Strawberry Shortcake

Fresh Raspberries or Strawberries sprinkled with fine sugar may be used as a filling between two rounds of the shortcake. Extra care must be taken when cutting.

235 Apple Shortcake

Well reduced stewed apple may also be used as a filling provided that it is drained of all syrup, cooked with an aromatic note of clove and coarsely chopped.

236 Poires d'Arenburg

Cut pear-shaped pieces of Genoese (see page 157) and make a small depression to accommodate a poached pear. The seeds may be removed from the end by means of a small vegetable scoop and the cavity filled with red currant jelly. Cover with Sauce d'Arenburg and pipe a spiral, a squiggle or what you will from a paper cornet filled with red currant jelly.

237 *Sauce d'Arenburg*

Use one part Crème Pâtissière (see page 129) to two parts of Custard Sauce, made in the proportions of 3 pints of milk, 1 lb. sugar and 12 yolks. Mix together and use when quite cold as sauce for the Poires d'Arenburg.

238 Pêches d'Arenburg

Peaches are prepared as indicated for Poires d'Arenburg.

239 Fresh Fruit Pancakes

Use pancakes made as described on page 137 and keep them in a pile with a cover over them. Have ready strawberries cut into convenient pieces, or raspberries, or ripe pears peeled and cut into a grosse julienne, or loganberries or, in fact, any ripe fruit that can be sweetened with a sugar syrup. Fold the fruit, whole or in convenient pieces into pancakes, heat on the service dish in the oven, sauce over with thick sweetened cream and send to the table.

240 Poires Gratinées

Chill some whole cooked peeled pears and roll them in a mixture of crushed almond macaroons and cake crumbs. Dress them on ovals of Genoese, in which you have carved a slight depression so that they do not roll about. At the last moment pop them under the griller to brown slightly.

241 Ananas Flambé au Kirsch

Cut thin rings from a trimmed pineapple, or if you are using canned pineapple rings, slice each ring into two. Fry each slightly in butter, dish up on silver flat, sprinkle with fine sugar and a few drops of kirsch and blaze with proof whisky.

242 Abricots Méringués

Cut out as many rounds of Genoese as required with a 2½-in. round pastry cutter, and with a small knife make a small depression in each, in which you place a whole cooked apricot. Using a star tube in the savoy bag, cover these apricots with meringue and place half a glacé cherry on top. Dust with icing sugar and place the tray in a cool oven until the meringue is dry. Serve a boat of sauce made of the juice in which the apricots were cooked which has been thickened with a little arrowroot if necessary.

243 Pêches Cardinal

Remove the skins from the peaches by scalding them or if they are very ripe by rubbing them on a towel. Poach them in a light syrup, and when they are cold dress them on rounds of Genoese, in which a slight depression should be made to counteract any tendency to rock or roll. Sauce the peaches over completely with apricot jelly coloured with red colouring, and sprinkle with strip almonds. If desired decorate with whipped cream from a bag and tube.

244 Poires au Vin Rouge

Peel 18 pears leaving the stalks on. Pack them closely together on a plat sauté. Then pour over them a light syrup mixed with ½ bottle of red wine, some red colour, a few cloves and 1-in. stick of cinnamon. Put a lid on the plat sauté and cook the pears gently, turning any that have escaped the red colour. It is best to keep the pears in the cooking liquor.

245 Poires Colbert

Peel the pears and poach them in simple syrup, i.e. 3 lb. lump sugar to 1 quart of water, brought to the boil and skimmed. When cold, dish the pears in individual dishes on a bed of crème pâtissière. Sauce over with thinned whipped cream, decorate with red currant jelly piped from a paper cornet and sprinkle a pinch of chopped pistachio on top.

246 Poires Mariette

Poach peeled pears in syrup and when they are cold dress them upright on a round of Genoese on which a ring of chestnut purée mixed with whipped cream has been piped from a star tube. They should be masked with an apricot sauce flavoured with rum.

247 Pommes Mariette

Apples peeled, cored and carefully cooked may be served in the same way. Select a variety which does not fall easily.

248 Pommes Méringuées

Peel and core the apples, cook them under cover and stand them on a round of Genoese when cold enough to move. Furnish a savoy bag with a ¼ in. plain tube, fill it with meringue and starting at the base pipe rings round the apples. Finish with a little cup on the top. Sugar the meringued apples with caster sugar and put them into a very cool oven or better into a drying oven. To serve, the apples should be lifted very carefully on to the serving dish and the cup on the top filled with red currant jelly.

249 Apricot, Pineapple or Pear Condé

Prepare *Riz Condé* by putting on to boil 3½ pints of milk with 10 oz. of sugar and 4 oz. butter. Add a pinch of salt, a piece of lemon peel or a bay-leaf or two and 18 oz. Carolina rice which has been well washed in two changes of warm water and drained. Bring this to the boil, cover the pan with a sheet of greased paper, then with a tightly-fitting lid, put into the oven. Allow 25 or 30 minutes for the cooking, testing at the end of that time by squeezing a grain of the rice between thumb and forefinger. Allow to cool slightly before whisking in vigorously 16 egg yolks.

Next mould into shapes to accommodate the fruit; round for the apricot halves, oval for the halves of pear and triangular or semicircular for the pineapple according to shape. Place the fruit in position and sauce with apricot sauce. Decorate with pieces of glacé cherries and lozenge shapes of angelica or other preserved fruit, according to fancy.

250 *Apricot Sauce*

Spanish apricot pulp is available in 2½ lb. and 10 lb. tins and is useful for the filling of apricot pies, for making apricot ice-cream or for apricot jam. It is the last of these which interests us at the moment. Either push the can of pulp through the sieve or better put it through the liquidizer; but be on the look-out for any odd fruit stone, which would be disastrous to the cutters of the machine. For jam take an equal quantity of granulated sugar, mix well together, place in a thick-bottomed pan and bring to the boil, stirring all the time with a wooden spatula, or it may stick and burn on the bottom. Cook to 230° F. (or what was called the Thread degree), clear away in stoneware jars and twist a piece of paper on top of each to keep the contents dust-free.

This jam, when let down with syrup or water, makes a very useful sauce (or pastry-cooks' standby) either plain or coloured red.

251 Bananes Négus

Slice bananas in two lengthwise and allowing three of these per person, soak them in a mixture of orange juice and rum. Dress these on ¼-in. thick pieces of Genoese cut to shape. Cover them with chocolate sauce and sprinkle with chopped almonds.

252 Gooseberry Fool

Put 1 quart of green gooseberries on to boil with about ½ pint of water and ½ lb. of granulated sugar. Cook them slowly, stirring frequently. When they are quite cooked pass them through a sieve and verify the sweetness, adding more fine sugar if needed. Leave to get quite cold and add 1 pint of whipped cream just prior to serving. Serve in individual ice glasses.

253 Fraises Romanoff

Chill the strawberries in a mixture of orange juice and Curaçao.

When required for service, dish them in a crystal bowl which has been kept in a refrigerator long enough to chill thoroughly and pipe whipped cream over them from a bag fitted with a star tube.

254 Macédoine de Fruits Frais Rafraîchis

Any fresh fruit in season may be used for this dish. Apples should be peeled thinly, cut into four and cored, then sliced. Bananas, peeled and either cut across in ¼-in. slices; or if a finger is pushed into the end of a peeled banana the fruit will split into its natural three divisions, these may then be cut across into ½-in. pieces. Red currants should be strigged and used as they are. Grapes should be peeled then stoned by means of a loop of wire (as described on page 47). Oranges peeled to the quick have the sections cut from the enveloping membranes and any pips removed. Peaches are peeled then cut into slices (about ¼-in. thick at the centre of the slice). Pears are peeled, cut into four, cored, then either cubed if long or cut into thickish slices. Pineapples should be peeled then cut lengthwise into eight and each eighth cut across into thin slices. Raspberries should be used as they are. Strawberries, if large, should be cut.

These fruits should be kept in the refrigerator in an earthenware bowl as some varieties do not tolerate contact with metal. Season with sugar and squeeze the juice of a lemon over them.

255 Coupe Mousseuse de Fruits Frais

Make a macédoine of fresh fruits in season, the more mixed the better. Grapes, ripe gooseberries, small strawberries and raspberries may be left whole. Cherries should be stoned; peaches and apricots stoned, skinned and sliced; pears, apples, oranges, bananas, mandarins or melons peeled and either sliced, cubed or cut into quarters.

Use champagne glasses, either the flat kind or the taller tulip-shaped ones. It is well to ice the fruit or, having filled the glasses, to keep them in the refrigerator until required. When this moment arrives, fill the glasses with a white sparkling wine which itself should have been on ice—and it need not be an expensive champagne.

256 Fruits Rafraîchis (1)

Put the required quantity of hulled strawberries to chill in the refrigerator. Take an equal amount of raspberries and half the amount of ripe red currants, crush them and strain off the juice. Sweeten this with sugar and flavour it with a glass of Kirsch and half a glass of Maraschino. Pour this over the strawberries and keep in the chill until required for service.

Fruits Rafraîchis (2)

Take stoned cherries and thin slices of ripe pineapple cut into six pieces and chill them in orange juice.

Fruits Rafraîchis (3)

Add to about 1 pint plain syrup (of the proportion 3 lb. of loaf sugar and 1 quart water boiled together) the juice of 2 oranges and 1 lemon, and the zest of all. Immerse fresh, clean strawberries in this syrup and put to chill in the refrigerator.

257 Eton Mess

Put the hulled strawberries into an earthenware basin, if they are big, cut them in half. Then squash them with the back of a fork. Do not attempt to reduce them into a purée. Add an equal volume of sweetened whipped cream to the berries and mix carefully. Dish into chilled crystal bowls.

258 Black Currant Whip

Pass cooked black currants through a sieve, preferably a hair sieve as the seeds in black currants are tiny. Mix the purée obtained with sweetened whipped cream and serve in glasses with Savoy biscuits.

ICE CREAM, ICES AND ICE PUDDINGS

If you contemplate a big demand for ice-cream I advise the purchase of an ice-cream-making machine with a built-in conservator for at least four varieties. This will enable you to make and store ice puddings to cope with any emergency, and have available a variety of cream or fruit ices for your table d'hote or à la carte service.

In addition to the cream ices (Vanilla, Chocolate and Coffee listed below) at Fortingall we always had fruit ices such as Banana or Apricot made according to the recipe which follows. In the season we used Raspberry and Strawberry, sieved to extract the seeds, and when available Black Currant and Gooseberry, both cooked before being passed through the sieve. A touch of red colour is needed in the Strawberry and of green in the Gooseberry.

259 Basic Recipe for Fruit Ices

1 pint Fruit Pulp
1½ pints Milk
13 oz. Sugar
Juice 1 lemon
White 1 Egg

Simply mix together and freeze.

260 Basic Recipe for Vanilla Ice

4 pints Milk
16 Yolks
20 oz. Sugar
Vanilla Essence

Put milk on to boil. Mix the yolks and sugar together and when the milk boils whisk it into the yolks. Tip the mixture back into the pan and cook, stirring briskly, until the first signs of boiling show, when the custard should be transferred to a cold bowl. Stir frequently to prevent the formation of a skin. Add vanilla essence to taste before freezing.

261 Chocolate Cream Ice

3 oz. Cocoa
⅔ pint Water
4 oz. Sugar
Vanilla Ice

Boil these together and when cold mix with half the above quantity of vanilla ice, and freeze.

262 Coffee Ice

Use any of the instant coffee powders on the market, mix with the Vanilla Ice recipe until the desired flavour is attained, then freeze.

263 Omelette Soufflée My Lord

Take an omelette-shaped piece of Genoese about ½ in. in thickness and anchor it with a smear of jam on a long oval dish. Arrange scoops of vanilla ice carefully on the cake and over them halves of cooked pears. Cover the whole with meringue, smooth the sides and top, pipe a border from a star tube on top and bottom, and add a little decoration—or if appropriate an inscription such as 'Happy Birthday' or 'Many Happy Returns'. Dust with icing sugar and brown lightly in a very hot oven.

264 Omelette Soufflée Milady

As the last, substituting cooked peaches for the pears.

265 Soufflé Paquita

Use a round dish with a circle of Genoese upon it; and on this put scoops of ice of the desired flavour, covered with well-drained macédoine of fruit. Mask with a firm meringue, which is best done from a bag and star tube. They may be decorated or left plain and a hollow rosette piped on top to be filled with brandy cherries when the soufflé is taken from the oven.

266 Omelette en Surprise, or Baked Alaska

Place an oval of Genoese on a long silver dish, anchoring it with a splash of jam or meringue. Arrange on top portions of the glaces asked for and cover with meringue. Use any surplus meringue for borders and décor around the sides. Dust with icing sugar and make a depression in the top to facilitate the baking of the meringue.

It is as well to keep a small plank of wood about 1 in. thick and say 12 in. long by 6 in. wide for use when any of these dishes with a filling of ice-cream. Soak this in water. The silver dish is placed on the wood on a baking sheet before putting it in the oven. Although the ice-cream is placed on the foundation of Genoese, the soaked wood does help in insulating the dish from the heat of the oven.

267 Soufflé Volcano

Place a round slice of Genoese on a silver or fireproof dish and on this build a compact mass of scoops of vanilla and strawberry ice (or any others preferred by the guest). Surround the side with a fairly thick layer of meringue, place a small round of Genoese on the top and cover this too with a layer of meringue. Pipe a star border around both top and bottom, dust with icing sugar and give the dish a flash in a hot oven. On removal fill the depression with brandy cherries and blaze with proof whisky.

268 Glace au Four

Place a scoopful of the ice required on a round of Genoese. Cover this carefully with meringue from a ¼-in. pipe, dust with sugar and flash in a hot oven.

269 Meringue Shells

Grease some clean baking-sheets with butter and dust them liberally with flour. Reverse the trays on the table and bounce them about to ensure that there is no loose flour left on them. Then, with a bag furnished with a ¾-in. round tube, pipe out meringues the size of half a duck's egg. It would be so easy to show you how to do this without leaving a long 'tail', but impossible to describe. Put the baking-sheets into an oven, warm but not hot, one that has been used for roasting earlier, and leave for twelve hours.

270 Pouding Glacé Montmorency

Chill thoroughly an ice-pudding mould either in the deep-freeze or in the ice-cream-making compartment of the freezer. Line this mould quickly with a ½-in. thick lining of vanilla cream ice and fill the interior with stoned, cooked cherries mixed with

left: Poires Colbert

centre: Glace au Four (with portion removed)

right: Poires Colbert

more vanilla ice and flavoured with a little Cherry Brandy. This filling should be prepared beforehand and kept in the freezer. Put a paper on the top and replace the lid, then push the mould in the coldest place you have, the bottom of the deep-freeze, for example, and leave it undisturbed until wanted.

When the moment arrives have ready a cold dish, put the mould in cold water for a moment, reverse the dish on the top of the mould and holding it firmly in place turn the two over giving a shake when the mould should leave the ice cleanly. A rosette of cream may now be piped on top of the pudding and a small pile of chilled cherries built on the top, or small rosettes of whipped cream may be piped around the base of the mould and a cherry placed on each.

271 Pêche Melba

If the peaches are fully ripe, wipe off the skins in a towel, but if not poach them in a light syrup before peeling and allowing them to become quite cold. Dress on vanilla ice and cover with Sauce Melba. Whipped cream may be used to decorate the dish.

272 *Sauce Melba*

Pass 3 lb. raspberry pulp through a fine sieve (to remove the seeds) and mix it with the same amount of red currant jelly and 2 lb. caster sugar. Mix well together with a wooden spoon, and mix repeatedly until the sugar has dissolved for it tends to fall to the bottom of the basin. Use a little Bush's red colour as the raspberry pulp inclines to a purple tint.

273 Poires Melba

Peel the pears, leave on the stalk, and poach them in a simple syrup. When cold dish them up as above for Pêche Melba.

274 Poires Fortingall

Poach the peeled pears in simple syrup and chill them. To serve, place a scoop of chocolate ice in a chilled ice dish, arrange a pear on top, cover with thinned Crème Chiboust and sprinkle a pinch of chopped pistachio over.

275 Pêches Tetrazzini

Put a scoop of raspberry ice on each coupe, which whether glass or metal should have been chilled for some time—if not, an accident is almost sure to happen when the weight of the peach on top makes the dish top-heavy. Cover the peach with an apricot mousseline, i.e. a little sieved apricot jam mixed into whipped cream. Pipe a rosette of plain whipped cream on top from a star tube and sprinkle a pinch of crushed pralin over.

276 Abricots Marquise

Put a scoop of apricot ice into a chilled metal or glass ice-cream coupe and on it place a cooked whole apricot. Cover with half-whipped cream and sprinkle chocolate shavings over.

277 *Chocolate Shavings*

Break up a tablet or two of eating chocolate and melt it slowly in a water-bath. Pour it on to a clean place on the marble slab. Allow it to cool but not harden. Take your largest cook's knife and anchor the end under your left hand, then with your right hand shave the surface of the chocolate lightly with the knife blade. If the temperature of the chocolate is correct you will get little rolls about 2 in. long exactly like those from a joiner's plane. When they are cold and hard they may be stored in a covered tin box lined with paper.

278 Coupe Singapour

Put a scoop of coffee ice into the chilled coupe, surmount this by a very thin slice of pineapple. Sauce this over with a thin cream seasoned with ground ginger, pipe a star of whipped cream on top and decorate it with a slice of preserved ginger.

279 Coupe Jacques

There are many variants of the way to dress this sweet; the classic one specifies half lemon ice and half strawberry ice with a Kirsch-flavoured macédoine of fresh fruits (the more varied the better) placed in the bottom of the coupe and the sole décor, a single black grape, perched on top. Some practitioners admit that whipped cream may be allowed as a final touch; but the dish when properly served is a long way from the can of chopped mixed fruit with a scoop of vanilla ice and a blob of whipped so-called 'cream' on top, surmounted by half a glacé cherry, which is sometimes offered.

280 Coupe Elizabeth

The true Coupe Elizabeth is made by garnishing an ice coupe with poached cherries macerated in Kirsch and Cherry Brandy, covering with a vanilla ice and decorating with whipped cream, then sprinkling a minute quantity of ground cinnamon over. This is best done by mixing the cinnamon intimately with a greater quantity of icing sugar and dusting this mixture over the ice from a sugar dredger.

281 Coupe Régence

Put a scoop of apricot ice in an ice coupe and place thereon a whole cooked apricot. Cover with half-whipped cream flavoured with Kirsch and sprinkle crystallized violets over.

282 Méringues Glacées

Sandwich two meringue shells together with a scoop of the selected ice and serve in a paper case. It is preferable to place the meringues so that the ice is showing, i.e. on their sides.

283 Poires Hélène

Place a peeled cooked pear on top of a scoop of vanilla cream ice in a chilled glass or metal coupe, and cover it with cold chocolate sauce.

284 Ice Puddings

The making of ice puddings is, in this present age of mechanical refrigeration, child's play. One has only to make three or four different flavoured ices, store them either in the ice-cream-making machine or in a deep-freeze and one is ready for the making of any ice pudding. The modern ice-pudding mould is a truncated cone with a domed top—the base being about 4 in. in diameter. It holds sufficient ice for eight portions. If you have any of the beautifully made pewter ice-pudding moulds and wish to use them, remember that the joints between the top and the middle and the bottom and the middle must be made waterproof with a smear of lard, if you immerse them in a bucket of a freezing mixture of salt and crushed ice. This does not arise, of course, if you keep your ice puddings in a deep freeze.

To unmould it is only necessary to immerse the mould in cold water for a moment, dry the exterior roughly with a cloth, remove the lid, reverse the mould on to the service dish (which should also be chilled), give it a shake and the mould should come away easily. In the case of the pewter moulds it is also necessary to remove the top or an air-lock may form and hinder the unmoulding.

285 Vacherin aux Fraises

Sometimes you may have surplus cold meringue to dispose of. That is the time to make a stock of meringue rings of various diameters which may be kept for an emergency. On a sheet of slightly greased grease-proof paper, pencil the outline of patty pans for individual sweets and small cake tins for larger numbers. With the meringue in a savoy bag fitted with a star tube, pipe rings the size of your pencilled circles making them two rounds high. Dry these all night in an oven which has been used during the evening for roasting and is still warm but not hot.

When the time comes to dress this sweet, remove the meringue ring from the paper carefully (if it breaks it is easily mended with a little whipped cream) and sit it on a disc of the same size cut from a sheet of Swiss Roll Sponge. Place this on a metal dish and fill the centre with hulled strawberries which have been macerated in liqueur; Kirsch, Curaçao, Brandy, Maraschino or a mixture of any of these.

286 Vacherin à l'Orange

Proceed as above but fill the vacherin with whipped cream flavoured with orange Curaçao and on top arrange orange sections peeled 'to the quick'; or the shape may be filled with orange or vanilla ice.

SUNDRY SWEETS

287 Kirschen Kuchen

Make a light cake batter by mixing—in the cake machine—1 lb. butter, 1 lb. caster sugar, 8 yolks and 4 eggs. Then stir in lightly by hand 14 oz. of flour. Put rounds of grease-proof paper in the bottoms of nine 6-in. sandwich pans and divide the mixture equally. Then spread it, leaving a depression in the centre of each by drawing the mixture up the sides. (This will give you a level top when the cakes are baked.) Now divide each kuchen into four with 4 cherries, using either drained cooked fresh red ones or canned cherries. Next put a cherry on each side of these markers, 2 in front of them and 1 at the point, giving four groups of 6 cherries with space between for cutting later. Bake these cakes in a moderate oven, allow them to cool. Pass a knife around the sides of the tins and turn out upside down. Having removed paper dust them with icing sugar from the sugar dredger and cut each into four portions in the spaces left between the groups of cherries.

288 Weinbeeren Kuchen

This is a similar sweet to the above, using ripe white grapes instead of cherries. A bowl of cream may be served with advantage to accompany this and the foregoing sweet.

289 Trifle

Save all the cuttings from sponge cakes, trimmings from Swiss roll, stale sponge finger biscuits or Genoese and cut them into small pieces before allowing them to become quite stale. Then put the lot into a mixing bowl and pour over a bottle of Sherry, which need not be one of the best nor should it be what is known as 'cooking sherry'. The best plan is to collect all the bottoms of Sherry, Madeira or Marsala bottles, and when you have collected about three parts of a bottle, decant the clear wine from the sediment, straining it through a piece of tammy cloth or a pad of muslin. To this may be added half the quantity in sweet Spanish wine. A few Ratafia biscuits should also be added and as these are expensive to buy there is no reason why you should not be your own supplier.

To serve trifle in individual portions an ice-cream 'disher' is the tool to use. Deposit the portions in individual glass coupes and surmount them with a rosette of whipped cream flavoured with a little brandy and piped from a star tube; decorate as desired with cherries and angelica or with crystallized violets, rose petals or orange flowers.

If you have to make a 'party' trifle, do so in a round crystal dish building it up into a dome. Cover this with whipped, flavoured cream by piping it from a bag and star tube in diminishing circles from the base upwards. Then smooth it over with a palette knife and proceed to apply any decoration desired from the star tube. Supplement this with glacé cherries, other fruits or crystallized flower petals. The one thing to avoid is a custard of any kind, especially one made with so-called custard powder.

290 *Ratafia Biscuits*

Weigh into a mixing bowl ½ lb. ground almonds, 1 oz. ground rice, 1 lb. fine grained granulated sugar, and sufficient unbeaten egg-whites to make the mixture of the proper consistency (this may be 3 or 4 according to the size of the eggs). Add a few drops of almond essence, and before you pipe out the whole of the mix, make a trial of 2 or 3. Use a clean oiled baking sheet dusted with flour and a piping bag fitted with a ¼-in. plain tube. Make the tiny macaroons no bigger than a sixpenny piece, and bake them in a cool oven. If they run out too flat, add a little more almonds and sugar; if they tend to blow up and crack add a little more white of egg. As advised above a few of these tiny macaroons are a great improvement in a trifle.

291 Diplomat Pudding

Make this with similar materials as for a trifle, though cubes of fruit cake may be included. Use buttered dariole moulds. Put ½ glacé cherry at the bottom and fill up the mould with cubes of Swiss roll, ends of Genoese and so on. If you use fruit cake be sure to cut off the brown baked edge. In filling, do not attempt to squeeze too much cake, etc., in, as room must be left for the custard. Sprinkle a few drops of Sherry on the cake filling and fill the moulds with the usual custard of 4 eggs to 1 pint of milk with a little sugar.

Stand the moulds in a baking dish with 1 in. of hot water in the bottom, bring the water to the boil on the stove, cover the puddings with a sheet of greased paper and put into the oven at a moderate heat. As soon as the custard is cooked remove the tray from the oven and store in the larder as it is, until wanted. For service the puddings should be heated in the moulds in a bath of hot water, unmouled on to the service dish and sauced over with a thin custard made with eggs. Diplomat Puddings are best if served straight from the oven, as they tend to *souffler*.

292 Crème Régence

Take 7 oz. stale sponge-cake crumbs or broken Savoy biscuits or trimmings of Genoese, sprinkle them with Kirsch and Maraschino and soak them in 1¾ pints of milk. Tip this into your liquidizer, add 8 eggs and 10 yolks with 10 oz. sugar and a pinch of salt. Make into a cream. Butter a quart size charlotte mould or two shallower ones of greater diameter, pour in the crème and cook in a steamer. It will help in the unmoulding if a round piece of buttered paper is placed in the bottom of the mould. When the crèmes are dished, they should have a ring of cooked apricots placed around the outside with a glacé cherry on each, or if halves of apricots are used, in the middle of each half. When served the dish should be sauced with Apricot Sauce.

293 Baba au Rhum

Make a little ferment in a 7 lb. jam jar with a ¼ pint milk, 1 oz. of yeast and ½ oz. sugar. Put this in a warm place and cover the jar with a cloth. When this ferment has risen and 'dropped' have ready 1 lb. flour which has been kept warm in the mixing bowl with ½ oz. sugar and a pinch of salt. Make all into a dough, adding 8 eggs and ½ lb. of melted butter. Many pastry-cooks add 4 oz. of washed currants to this mixing, but it is a matter of personal choice. Allow the dough to ferment in the mixing bowl, covered with a cloth to keep off draughts, until well risen. Meantime prepare the small aluminium pudding bowls by greasing them with clarified butter. Knock back the dough, i.e. work it until the gas is out of it. Fill the prepared moulds one-third full with the baba dough and put them into a warm place or a very cool oven until they have risen to two-thirds of the height of the moulds. Bake them in a moderate oven, when they should fill the moulds to the top. When they are cold, store them in a cool larder until wanted; they will keep for weeks if dry. Do not take them out of the moulds until wanted.

294 To serve Baba au Rhum

First make a syrup by boiling together 4 lb. granulated sugar with 4½ pints of water, skimming it and passing it through a fine strainer. This will keep in a cool larder almost indefinitely and requires to be brought to boiling point when soaking the babas. It does not make any difference how dried up the babas may be provided that they are not mouldy, as they will recover their bulk in the hot syrup. A few drops of rum are sprinkled on the top of each prior to service, and a brandy cherry held by its stalk pushed into the top.

295 *Brandy Cherries*

Morello cherries are used, the stalk shortened to 1 in. Pack them into fruit-preserving jars of the kind with a glass lid held down on to a rubber ring by a metal clip, or a metal ring with a thread which engages with a similar one cast on the neck of the bottle. With the fruit stowed in the jars add fine sugar to fill them one-quarter full. Then fill them with gin, place the lid in position and clip down, or screw down, and shake periodically. You may think it fraudulent to substitute gin for brandy, but think of the difference in cost. In any case you are not selling gin as brandy. No doubt vodka could be used as it is a tasteless spirit; I have not experimented with it.

296 Baba (Large)

Baba may also be made in large size moulds, about 7 in. tall and 4 in. in diameter at the open end. Fill these one-third full with baba dough, allow to prove to two-thirds height and bake. Do not remove from the mould until quite cold. With the baba still in the mould and using a long slender knife, cut out a plug from the centre leaving a wall ½ in. thick. In order to free this plug, insert a small sharp knife about ½ in. from the bottom of the baba and make a cut across without enlarging the opening at point of insertion. With luck and on reversing the baba the plug should fall out.

The baba may now be filled with a compote of cherries, the syrup of which has been thickened slightly with arrowroot. Put about 3 cherries at the bottom of the baba shell and cut a piece about 1 in. long from the plug. Fit this over the cherries and continue with more cherries and more slices from the plug until the centre is filled. The exterior of the baba should be brushed with boiling apricot jelly; and if the sweet is to be served at a *diner particulier* it should be sent to the table blazing. The head waiter should be informed that when the flames have burnt out, the baba should be put on its side and served from that position. In place of cherries other fruits may be used as filling for a baba such as a compote of pineapple cut into small cubes and flavoured with rum, or compote of fresh peaches or fresh apricots, either of which may be seasoned with an appropriate liqueur.

297 Savarins

These are made from baba dough in round or oval Savarin moulds. These should be filled one-third full with baba dough and allowed to prove until two-thirds full before being baked. When cool and unmoulded soak them in hot syrup, splash them with an appropriate liqueur and brush them over with hot apricot jelly. The centre may be filled with whipped cream piped from a star tube and a garnish of cooked fresh apricots placed over it. Rosettes of whipped cream decorated with glacé cherries and leaves cut from angelica should adorn the ring of the savarin. The liqueur used should be apricot brandy.

The rings or ovals of savarins may be used as above to accommodate quarters of cooked fresh peaches, in which case peach brandy should be used as the flavouring liqueur.

298 Oeufs à la Neige

These are made by poaching the meringue mixture. Prepare some large sauté pans by greasing them with butter. Chill them and pipe oval meringue shapes on to them from a ¾-in. pipe. Have some hot milk waiting and ladle in sufficient of this to float the meringues comfortably. Allow them to poach on the stove for a minute or two then turn over with a spoon or skimmer to finish the cooking. Remove them with a skimmer and arrange them for service in glass dishes, two per portion.

Next measure the cooking milk and make it into a coating custard with sufficient of the yolks you have on hand from the meringue. Flavour this with vanilla and when cold, sauce over the cooked meringues you have arranged on the glass dishes.

299 Zambaglione

Put 6 yolks with ½ pint of Marsala into a *bassin à blancs* and beat until as light as possible over hot water. Meantime put the 6 whites with 8 oz. of sugar into the egg-whisking machine and beat into a light meringue. Blend the two together carefully. Serve in glass coupes. A few fraises de bois may be sprinkled on top.

This is also known as *Zabaione* or *Sabayon.*

300 Steamed Orange Pudding

Weigh 10 oz. of table margarine into the bowl of the cake-mixing machine and add 10 oz. fine sugar. Warm these together so that they will cream up lightly. Add the finely-chopped zest of an orange, put in the beater and beat up to a light cream adding 5 eggs one at a time whilst doing so. Meantime sieve together 10 oz. rice flour, 2 oz. plain flour and 1 teaspoonful of baking powder. Stir this into the mix on slow speed.

Have ready 18 or 20 dariole moulds (individual pudding size) greased with butter, and half fill them with the mixture. Plaster it well up the sides so that the finished puddings will be level on top. Twist a piece of grease-proof paper over the top of each or invert a clean patty-pan to cover. Next put them in the steamer and cook for ¾ hour. Over-cooking will not harm them and they may be re-warmed when required without the loss of quality.

For the sauce, strain some marmalade, add a little water and thicken slightly with arrowroot.

301 Ginger Pudding

Make up the mix as given for steamed orange pudding substituting a heaped teaspoonful of ground ginger for the chopped zest of an orange. The sauce should be an ordinary sweet white sauce with a flavouring of ginger and a slight colouring of caramel or gravy browning.

302 Steamed Fruit Puddings

Put 18 oz. flour into the mixing machine with 1 teaspoonful of baking powder, 6 oz. sugar, 6 oz. margarine, 3 eggs and ¾ pint or less of milk. Knock this up into a smooth batter. Next butter the number of individual pudding moulds required, smearing the batter around bottom and sides in an even layer. (Note: the mixture must have enough body to stay where it is put on the sides of the moulds and not slip to the bottom.) Remember to save sufficient of the batter to cover the puddings when they are filled.

A large Victoria plum would fill one of the lined moulds; so use small fruit, black currants, cherries, plums, damsons, small gooseberries (the cooking variety), bilberries, raspberries. One must remember that fruit shrinks on cooking, so it must be well tassed down in the moulds, or even allowed to stand slightly above the top of the mould. This will give a slight domed effect when the mould is roofed over with a round of the batter, but it will disappear in cooking. A little sugar should be allowed to drop among the fruit before sealing on the lid.

Steam these little puddings as instructed above and serve with a suitable sauce. Use one made from the juice of the fruit concerned, or a custard sauce if preferred.

303 Omelette au Rhum

Make an omelette in the usual way and when it is on the service dish sprinkle it with caster sugar and blaze it with proof rum.

304 Omelette Noël

Make the omelette and before folding it spread a spoonful of heated mincemeat along the centre, then turn it out on to the dish, sugar it and blaze it with proof rum.

PASTRY

305 Short Crust

Put 4 lb. flour and 1¾ lb. neutral fat into the mixing bowl, put on the cake beater and mix on slow speed to a crumbly condition. Then add 1 pint of cold water, ¾ oz. fine salt and mix to a firm dough.

306 Chausson aux Pommes

Place a strip of short crust 4½ in. wide, the length of your baking sheet and on it spread a heaped layer of sliced apples (or sliced canned apples) sprinkled with either chopped orange zest or soaked sultana raisins. Season with sugar if necessary and cover with a thinner sheet of the same pastry. Trim the edges and make a pinched border on both sides. Put on one side to recover from any toughening you may have given to the pastry during handling and rolling out. Stab the covering layer of pastry here and there (or in a design) with a pointed knife and bake, first wetting the top surface and dusting with fine sugar.

Mixed fruit or apricots also make good Chaussons.

307 Yorkshire Apple Pie

This is made, as you all know, from cooking apples (preferably Bramley Seedling if you like a fruit that cooks into a pulp). These are peeled, cored and cut into pieces or sliced, and put into a pie-dish, with a clove at the bottom of the dish, and sugared. The fruit is roofed over with short crust which is then washed with water, dusted with fine sugar and, after the necessary period of rest, baked. I suggest that you make individual apple pies. You will find that the smallest size of Pyrex pie-dishes are admirable for this purpose.

308 Apple Pie: Variation 1

As a variation of the above, perhaps you will try something entirely different, which hails from either Poland or Russia. When the leaves on your black currant bushes are the size of a sixpenny piece, gather some of the buds and drop them into a bottle with 1 in. of gin in the bottom. When next you make an apple-pie put one of these buds in the bottom of the dish under the apples. Your guests will be intrigued by the new flavour.

309 Apple Pie: Variation 2

Another variation dates from the time when cloves or other spices were too scarce or too dear to buy. Smear the bottom of the pie-dish with a little finely chopped onion, in with the sugared apples, and before putting on the pastry lid sprinkle the contents with a little grated cheese.

310 Yorkshire Mint Pasty

Line a tin plate with a disc of short pastry and on it spread a mixture of currants, raisins (stoned if necessary) and finely chopped mixed orange and lemon peel, mixed with Demerara sugar. Over this sprinkle chopped mint leaves with more currants, etc., on top. Season with ground spice, wet the edges of the pastry with water and put another round of the pastry on top. Seal the two layers of pastry together with a pinched border, brush over with a wetted brush and sprinkle with sugar. Make a few cuts here and there and bake.

311 German Dough

Mix 2 lb. butter, 1¼ lb. caster sugar and 8 eggs into a batter in the cake machine, then stir in on slow speed 3½ lb. flour with ½ lb. ground almonds to make a firm dough. Smaller quantities can be made in proportion. Wrapped in foil this keeps well in a refrigerator, but do not freeze.

312 Bandeaux aux Abricots

Roll out a strip of German dough ¼ in. thick and 4½ in. wide on your baking sheet. Allow this to lie for a quarter of an hour, then stab with a skewer and bake. When cool, pipe a rope border of meringue on the edges from a bag and star tube. Allow this to set in a *very cool* oven. When quite cold, arrange drained halves of apricots across the strip: it will take about three halves per portion, but put them neatly so that you can cut the sweet into slices without disarranging the fruit. From the drained syrup and a little added sugar make a sauce which will jell when cold, and brush this over the fruit whilst still hot. This is a sweet which may be served cold or warm; but as the pastry is very fragile the portions should be cut from it on the baking sheet.

313 Bandeau Méringué aux Marrons

Run out a strip of German dough on a baking sheet, stab it and bake. When cool pipe a border of meringue from a star tube on each side, which you may either dry in a cool oven or toast slightly in a hotter one. Fill the middle of the strip with a fifty/fifty mixture of whipped cream and crème de marrons and on it place halves of marrons preserved in syrup. Cut across into appropriate slices.

314 Flan aux Abricots

Line a 9-in. flan ring with short-crust pastry and fill the bottom with drained halves of apricots. Bake this and when cool cover with a jelly made from the drained juice boiled with added sugar.

A more elaborate flan aux abricots can be made by stuffing the hollow of each ½ apricot with a ball of marzipan or almond paste the size of a small cherry; and when the flan is baked and cool, piping a border of meringue and a series of 'S' shapes (eight or nine in all) where the portions will be cut. The meringue should be dried slightly before cutting.

315 Flan aux Abricots Méringué

This is a further elaboration and consists in covering the top surface of the baked flan with meringue which is then dried in a cool oven. If the top is smoothed with a wetted knife before drying, decoration may be applied later from a cornet of paper containing red currant jelly.

316 Flan aux Abricots (aux Fruits) à la Bourdaloue

This is a type of sweet which may be adapted to accommodate most fruits when in season. Ripe apricots, ripe greengages (not stoned and with the skin on), fresh raspberries or strawberries.

Short pastry flan-cases are baked blind in the usual manner.

top left:
Poires au vin rouge

top right:
Spritz Kuchen

centre:
Poires Hélène

bottom left:
Polka Créole

bottom right:
Bandeau aux Abricots Méringués

When they are ready, prepare a Crème Pâtissière and pour it into the baked cases. If the flans are to wait some time, a pat of butter rubbed over the surface of the custard will prevent a skin forming. Next arrange the fruits on the top of the Crème Pâtissière and cover them with apricot jelly. Sprinkle liberally with pralin. A 9-in. flan ring will yield eight portions.

317 *Crème Patissière*

Mix 4 oz. sugar and 2 oz. flour together and then beat in 4 yolks and 1 whole egg. Meanwhile put on ¾ pint of milk to boil. When ready pour this on to the sugar, flour and egg mixture, stirring briskly. Put this back on the stove and cook until the mixture is boiling.

318 *To make Pralin*

Put ¼ lb. granulated sugar into a copper skillet (see Glossary). If you do not possess such a pan, an untinned brass one will suit or an aluminium pan. The reason why I insist on the pan used not being tinned is that the heat at which tin melts is not far removed from that at which sugar does; and I am quite sure that you do not wish to have little bullets of tin spoil your pralin.

Having put the sugar on to heat in a suitable pan, stir it constantly with a wooden spatula or spoon, until it melts and takes on a golden tint. At this moment mix in 2 oz. of chopped almonds, stir together quickly and pour out on to an oiled part of the pastry slab or failing this use an oiled baking sheet. You will probably have met with a similar product under the name of 'Russian Toffee'. When the pralin is cold and hard, crush it under a rolling-pin and use as described.

It is not of any advantage to make a quantity of pralin as it tends to liquefy on keeping, but if you do have a surplus it is possible for you to keep it dry and free from moisture by wrapping it in a polythene bag and storing it in a very dry place.

319 Flan aux Poires à la Bourdaloue

Prepare flan-cases as above. Then peel pears and cook them whole in a simple syrup, allowing 8 pears per flan. When they are cool arrange them stalk end inwards on the crème pâtissière and cover with either melted red currant jelly or apricot jelly tinted red. Sprinkle with pralin as before.

320 Flan aux Cerises à la Bourdaloue *or* Flan aux Pêches à la Bourdaloue

These are made exactly the same way as Flan aux Abricots à la Bourdaloue.

321 Flan à ma Façon

Line 9-in. flan rings with short pastry and cover the bottom of each with a ¼-in. layer of mincemeat. Over this place a cake mixture of 6 oz. margarine, 6 oz. sugar, 2 eggs and 8 oz. flour with 3 oz. ground almonds, a pinch of baking powder, a drop or two of almond essence and sufficient milk to make a cake batter. Twice this mixture will be sufficient for three flans. When they are baked and cool, cut into eight portions (nine or ten if you are needing them, you will find they are still a good portion). Dust the tops with icing sugar and serve.

322 Mince Pie

You have the choice of two alternatives; either make individual pies or plate pies, cutting them into eight or more portions.

(*a*) For the former line patty pans with rounds of thin short paste and thumb well out. (This is a difficult operation to explain and consists in pressing out the bottom of the pastry thinly with the thumbs—any pastry-cook will, I am sure, give a demonstration.) Fill these lined patty pans with a good ball of mince-meat each, splash them with water and cover them with lids of puff pasty $\frac{3}{16}$ in. thick. Press these well down on to the pastry bases and stab the tops with a knife. When baked and cool dust with icing sugar.

(*b*) For a plate mince pie, use a metal pie plate the size of a dinner plate and cover it with a sheet of short paste. On this spread a layer of mince-meat and over it, having sprinkled a few drops of rum, place another sheet of short paste. Seal the edges with a pinched or notched border, make a few cuts with a knife on the top, wash with water and sprinkle with caster sugar then bake.

323 Tarte aux Pommes (Puff Pastry)

Take a strip of puff pastry 3 in. wide and $\frac{3}{16}$ in. thick as long as your baking sheet. Now press the rolling-pin in the middle of this strip lengthwise and roll it slightly, giving a strip $4\frac{1}{2}$ in. wide with a thin middle and two borders $\frac{3}{16}$ in. thick. The result is as though you had rolled out a thin sheet of pastry and put a thicker piece one on each side, but with a great saving in time. Next peel the apples, cut them in halves and core them. Now slice them and arrange the slices across the flan strip slightly overlapping. After allowing time for the puff pastry to recover from the rolling, bake the strip and on removing from the oven, brush over with apricot jelly. To serve cut across the strip between the lines of apple slices.

Other fruit in season may be used: gooseberries, halved plums, ripe apricots, even raspberries and strawberries though these last are not too successful.

324 Tarte aux Fruits

Use a strip of German dough and either pinch the borders or run a thin strip of the dough down each side, or make the main strip thicker and slightly less wide, then pin out the centre as with the puff pastry above. Whichever way is chosen, stab the centre to prevent blisters and wash with beaten egg twice where the fruit will lie, then bake. When cool arrange the fruit neatly on the middle part and brush over with well-boiled apricot jelly coloured

red. This will hold the fruit in position and sweeten it at the same time. Cut the strips into portions on the baking sheet when cold, either with a knife or better a Scotch scraper.

325 Bakewell Tarts: Traditional Recipe

Line the required number of 6-in. sandwich tins with German dough and spread a thin layer of strawberry jam over the bottom of each. Weigh ¼ lb. butter into a pan, bring it to the boil and take off any scum. Meanwhile place 3 eggs and 1 yolk into a mixing bowl and beat them up with 4 oz. of caster sugar. Beat the boiling butter into this mixture well and place a thick layer over the jam. Bake in a moderate oven until pastry is baked and filling has a delicate brown tint. I know that it is usual to make individual tarts in patty pans; but the above method was adopted in my hotel to save labour, as it did not spoil the finished article in any way. When cool the tarts are cut into six portions. The recipe is a genuine old-fashioned Derbyshire speciality.

326 Bakewell Tarts (2)

Line three 6-in. sandwich tins as above with German dough and cover the bottoms with strawberry jam. Then prepare the following mixture as a cake batter: 4 oz. butter and 4 oz. caster sugar beaten together with 3 eggs. Mix in 6 oz. ground almonds with 2 oz. flour, 1 level teaspoonful of baking powder and a drop of almond essence. Cover the jam carefully with this mixture, smooth over with a palette knife and bake in a moderate oven. Each of the tarts will cut into six portions.

327 Lemon Meringue Pie

Line two 9-in. rings with short pastry and bake them blind. When they are nearly ready prepare the filling. First put 1½ pints of water on to boil, then mix 12 oz. sugar with 4 oz. cornflour and stir in 6 yolks with the juice and finely chopped zest of 2 lemons. Pour the boiling water on to this mixture, stirring briskly, then return to the pan. Continue the stirring until the mixture shows signs of boiling and divide it into the two flan-cases which by now should have suitably cooled.

Take 4 of the whites of the eggs and with 8 oz. sugar make a cold meringue which you pipe on to the top of the flans. After dusting them with fine sugar, give them a touch of colour in a cool oven. You may decorate the meringue with red currant jelly from a paper cornet, then cut each flan into eight portions.

328 California Raisin Pie

Cook two 9-in. flan-cases blind. Stew 1 lb. seedless raisins in 1 pint of water with 4 oz. sugar. When the raisins are soft, mix 1 oz. cornflour with a spoonful of water (to make it into a creamy mass), add the juice of 2 lemons and 2 beaten eggs and stir into the raisins. Cook this mixture for a few minutes, stirring briskly, then turn it into the empty flan-cases and level the top surfaces with a wetted knife. Cut each into eight portions.

329 Gâteau Mille Feuilles (Puff Pastry)

It is not proposed to tell you how to make puff pastry. Enemy though I am of all factory produced foodstuffs, I must admit that the puff pastry marketed by the firm of Jus-Rol Ltd., in Coldstream, is excellent. I have used their product since first I came to know of it and saved myself many hours of laborious work.

Roll out a sheet of puff pastry to about 3/16 in. in thickness and from it cut three bands 5 in. wide. Transfer these without stretching them on to a baking sheet, stab them and bake in a hot oven. When cool spread one band with Crème Chiboust flavoured with vanilla. Make the layer of Crème at least ½ in. in thickness. On this place another band of the cooked puff pastry and on it spread raspberry jam. Lastly place the third band of pastry on it, spread a layer of water icing and thereon sprinkle roasted flake almonds.

As a refinement, the side of the assembled gâteau may be evened slightly with a sharp knife, and then spread with a little of the surplus crème. Thereafter the crumbled trimmings can be used as a coating over this crème. The gâteau is then cut with a sharp knife into slices. At about 1½ in. in width the slice should stand upright on the guest's plate.

330 *Crème Chiboust*

Make the recipe for Crème Pâtissière (see page 000) and when it is boiling have ready 5 whites of egg and 1½ oz. caster sugar beaten into a firm meringue. Whilst one assistant is dealing with the crème pâtissière another should be attending to the meringue and shaking off portions from his whisk into the boiling crème. The process of mixing the two together must be done quickly for the whites are cooking in the hot custard, yet they must be thoroughly mixed. Do not overbeat or the cream will become liquid, lose quantity and be useless.

In addition to Gâteau Mille Feuilles, Crème Chiboust is used to fill éclairs, profiterolles, cream buns, polka vanille, polka créole.

CHOUX PASTRY

331 Profiterolles au Chocolat

Make a Pâte à Choux from 1 pint of milk, 10 oz. margarine, 10 oz. flour and 10 eggs. Put the milk and margarine on to boil and when they are doing so merrily get an assistant to tip the sieved flour in carefully whilst you stir vigorously—if not there will be lumps of uncooked flour to contend with. Whilst this is cooling slightly, prepare a baking sheet. You will need to cook under cover and I suggest a reversed roasting tin. Place the tin upside down on a baking sheet and dust the edge with flour. Remove the tin and you will see the area you have at your disposal for the profiterolles. Pipe these out in ¾-in. blobs of pâte à Choux, not forgetting to leave room for them to swell in baking. Splash these blobs with a little water, cover them with the roasting tin and bake in a fairly hot oven (380° F. or Mark 4–5). They must be quite dry, before being filled with vanilla-flavoured Crème Chiboust from a Savoy bag furnished with a ¼ in. tube. Push the tube into the profiterolles and squeeze sufficient cream from the bag you are holding in your right hand.

Profiterolles au Chocolat are prepared on demand by placing a layer of filled profiterolles in a glass dish and saucing them over with chocolate sauce, then arranging another layer over and covering it with the sauce, with perhaps a few more profiterolles to give the desired domed effect.

332 *Chocolate Sauce (cold mix)*

Mix 4 oz. cocoa with 4 oz. caster sugar and add sufficient cold milk to make a creamy consistency. This sauce will thicken on standing, so it should be thinned as required.

333 Spritz Kuchen

This is another good sweet made from pâte à Choux. Cut some sheets of grease-proof paper the size of your deep fat container, dip them in the fat and allow them to cool. Then, from a bag fitted with a star tube, pipe on the prepared paper 'figure eights' about 3½ in. long. When the frying fat is hot enough, lift up one of these papers by two corners and place it face down on the surface of the frying fat. The kuchen will free themselves and the paper may be removed and kept for future use. When the undersides of the kuchen are of a golden colour, turn them over with the skimmer and allow the frying to be completed. This done, remove them with a skimmer and allow to drain and cool. Next either dust them thickly with icing sugar and place them under the salamander for the sugar to caramelize slightly, or ice them with water icing.

As an alternative Spritz Kuchen may be piped out into rings 3 in. in diameter; subsequent treatment is as above.

334 Polka Vanille

Cut out a disc of short paste with a 9-in. flan ring, egg-wash the border and stab the middle with the point of a knife. On the border pipe pâte à choux from a ½-in. pipe and pipe another ring in the middle 4 in. in diameter. Egg-wash both rings and bake. When cool fill with vanilla-flavoured Crème Chiboust and smooth over, the centre ring being slightly higher. Dust well with caster sugar and, with a red-hot poker, make a criss-cross design of caramelized sugar.

335 Polka Créole

As above but without the ring in the centre. When the flan is filled, take 8 slices of pineapple and cut a little from two sides of each giving three-cornered pieces. Arrange these on the border and brush over with apricot jelly. Place a glacé cherry in the hole of each pineapple slice and sprinkle a pinch of chopped pistachio in the centre of the flan.

336 Bandeaux of Choux Pastry

Run out two strips of choux pastry the full length of a slightly greased oven sheet. Do this from a bag and ¾-in. plain tube, by piping four lines almost touching for each strip, then spread them flat and as evenly as possible with a wetted palette knife. Allow to rest, then bake in a hot oven (about 450° F.). When they are quite cold, the strips are sandwiched together as follows:

(*a*) Spread the tops of two strips with crème pâtissière, on one place sliced bananas and splash with rum. Turn the other over on to this making a sandwich. Press lightly and dust the top with icing sugar. Then either cut across into slices about 1½ in. wide or cut the assembled strips down the middle, then cut across into square pieces.

(*b*) Treat the two strips of baked choux pastry as above but cover one with thin slices of trimmed pineapple before making the sandwich.

(*c*) Fresh ripe fruit may be used, raspberries or sliced strawberries. Crème Chiboust should be used in both cases.

(*d*) Make a crème au beurre, flavour it with cocoa and heighten the colour with a drop or two of gravy browning. Use this thickly between the two strips of choux paste and make the sides even. Spread red currant jelly or raspberry jam on the top and sprinkle chopped almonds over.

(*e*) Make a crème au beurre au café. Do this by adding small quantities of one of the instant coffee powders on the market to the crème whilst it is being beaten in the machine, until the desired flavour is reached. Proceed as above and finish by dusting the top with icing sugar or, having spread it with a thin layer of the crème, sprinkling it with chocolate nonpareils or chocolate vermicelle.

PANCAKES

337 Thin Pancakes

Make a batter from 8 oz. flour, 2 eggs, 1 pint milk, and a pinch each of sugar and salt. Use small pancake pans about 5½ in. in diameter. One person can operate four of these and should get 40 pancakes from this mixture. A few drops of cooking oil are needed from time to time for greasing purposes. Oil pan number one, swill the oil around and tip it into pan number two. Put a small ladleful of batter into the first pan and tip the surplus (i.e. that which does not stick to the bottom) back into the basin. Proceed in like manner with the other pans, swilling the surplus oil from one pan to the next. Number one will be ready for tossing over by the time you arrive at number three. A few seconds and the first pancake can be placed on a plate and the pan is ready for the oil from number four. A gas stove is most suitable for this operation as the heat is so easily controlled. After a little practice you will get the rhythm and be able to make in a very short time the 40 pancakes which the above mix will produce.

In order to keep the pancakes moist they should be stacked in one heap with a basin over them as cover. If they are to be kept for a little time (à la carte work, for instance) they can be wrapped in foil; but they must be quite cold before being wrapped or they will become mouldy.

338 Crêpes aux Avelines

Roast hazel-nuts slightly to remove the skins and develop the flavour. Pound them in the mortar with a little sugar, or whizz them in the liquidizer, until they become a purée. Use this purée to flavour a crème au beurre (see page 159) with which you spread the pancakes. Roll these up and serve two per portion. Sprinkle them with fine sugar and surround the dish with thinned cream flavoured with Noyau.

339 Crêpes du Couvent

When making the pancakes, place thin slices of cooked pears on half each pancake, then fold over to cover them. Two of these folded pancakes make a portion. Sprinkle with sugar and surround the dish with thinned cream.

340 Crêpes Lady Curzon

Diced bananas are stewed gently with sugar in cream, to fill rolled pancakes which are blazed with rum.

341 Crêpes Normande

Fill the pancakes with apple purée mixed with cream and flavoured with Calvados. When dished sprinkle the pancakes with sugar and run a cordon of cream around them on the exposed parts of the dish.

342 Crêpes Singapour

Make the pancakes as usual, but do not toss. Place half a thin slice of pineapple in place and fold over, so that the pineapple is warmed in the pancake. Serve two per portion, place a slice of preserved ginger on each pancake and sauce the dish with cream flavoured with ginger syrup.

343 Crêpes Suzette

The abominations usually served to you in town restaurants as Crêpes Suzette have no relation to the real thing; but the method I offer you here does approximate more nearly to it.

To a mixing of Crème au Buerre, add the finely chopped zest of 2 oranges and flavour with a little Grand Marnier. When required for use, soften the amount needed and put a teaspoonful in the middle of each pancake. Fold in half and again in half, giving quadrants with the orange cream at the point. Now arrange these on the service dishes (two per portion) and put in a warm place awaiting service. When this moment arrives, warm sufficient proof whisky to cover the pancakes, ignite it and pour it over the dish. Send to the table at once.

344 Bananes Favorites

Peel some bananas and cut each across into two. Now push your forefinger carefully down each half and you will find that each will split into three natural divisions giving you six pieces of banana. Cook these carefully in butter, allowing two for each portion, and roll each in a pancake. Butter the service dishes and arrange the filled pancakes close together in a diamond shape. Have ready some meringue and cover the top surface smoothly with it, then pipe a border on it from a star tube. Place these dishes in a cool oven to dry the meringue slightly.

At the moment of service a little compote of chopped pineapple in apricot jelly should be spread on the top and the sweet may then be sent to the table as it is or blazed.

345 Crêpes Garnies de Confitures

Spread pancakes with a mixture of wild strawberry jam and pineapple jam cut into small dice, seasoned with a spot or two of *Kirsch* and *Curaçao*. Roll these and arrange them, two per portion on the service dishes. Have ready a Sabayon and spoon this over the pancakes. Dust lightly with icing sugar and brown in a hot oven. Send to table at once.

346 Flan Méringué à la St. Crevaz

This is also known as *Flan Méringué à la Crepazzi*. Make a pile of crêpes about 2 in. in height by sandwiching them with Crème Pâtissière, Crème Chiboust or a well-reduced fruit compote. Spread a stiff meringue on top and around the sides, sprinkle with chopped almonds, dust with icing sugar and brown slightly in the oven. Sauce the surround with Apricot Sauce or melted Red Currant Jelly.

347 Crêpes Soufflés

Put a spoonful of vanilla soufflé mixture (or any other desired flavour) in the middle of a crêpe and fold the sides over it. Butter a silver flat dish and arrange the stuffed pancakes on it alongside one another, two per portion, with the closing downwards. Dust them with caster sugar and bake them for a few minutes in a hot oven. If they are properly filled they will appear as fat cigars with the soufflé mixture peeping from the ends. Serve without delay, having run a little thinned cream of the same flavour as the soufflé mix around the exposed parts of the dish.

SOUFFLÉS

348 Vanilla Soufflé

You require ¾ pint of milk which you put on to boil with a piece of stick vanilla. Place in a basin 4 oz. caster sugar with 2 oz. flour and mix well, add 4 yolks and 1 whole egg and stir together. To this add the milk gradually until a smooth mass is obtained, then return it to the pan and bring it to the boil, stirring vigorously the while. Next whip 8 whites into a firm snow using 2 oz. sugar to help. Mix this lightly into the flour and egg paste and turn it into a soufflé mould which has been buttered and sugared. Fill to the top and level off with a knife.

Bake in a moderate oven until the soufflé has risen to half its height but no more. It may then be kept in a warm place until the moment of service arrives, when a few minutes in a hot oven will bring it up to its full height, i.e. double its original volume. Once this is reached it must be served at once for a soufflé that has fallen into a crumpled mass at the bottom of the mould is ruined. When I was an apprentice cook there was a saying to the effect that there were only two dishes that a guest must wait for—an omelette, which must go straight from stove to table, and a soufflé which must go straight from oven to table.

349 Soufflé Rothschilde

Make a soufflé pudding as for vanilla soufflé but in place of the vanilla add a salpicon of preserved fruits. When the soufflé is moulded, push in here and there ½-in. lengths of either Sponge Finger biscuits or Boudoir biscuits which have been soaked in Bénédictine Liqueur and bake.

350 Soufflé Irma

Take cooking apples of even size and with a pair of pliers remove the stalks. Verify that the apples will stand without rocking on the stalk end and then remove a slice from each a quarter of the way down from the flower end. Empty the apples of pulp by means of a large size vegetable scoop (the one used for Pommes Parisienne) taking care that the skin is not broken. Cook the pulp removed from the apples with a little sugar and a pat of butter, and pass it through a sieve to remove any bits of core or skin. Use this to cover the bottom of the inside of the apple skins. Make a meringue of ½ pint of whites and 1 lb. sugar and pipe from a ½-in. plain tube. This will cover thirty Soufflé Irma. Push 1-in. pieces of Savoy biscuit soaked in Kummel into the meringue and finish by piping a few blobs from the same tube on top. Dust with icing sugar and sprinkle a little grated chocolate over. Bake these in a moderate oven for about 5 minutes and if necessary sprinkle more icing sugar and grated chocolate over.

351 Soufflé à l'Orange en Surprise

This is a similar dish to the above. Prepare 4 oranges by cutting a slice from one end and emptying the fruit by cutting with a sharp knife near the skin, then taking out the pulp with a spoon. As oranges are apt to be somewhat unstable, in addition to cutting off a small slice from the now bottom end it is as well to seat each orange in a paper case to forestall any accidents by rocking. Put these orange shells into the deep freeze until required. At that moment have a small quantity of meringue ready, half fill the orange shells with vanilla ice (or any desired flavour), pipe over this with meringue from a ½-in. tube, dust with icing sugar and flash in a hot oven.

352 Pouding Soufflé au Citron

Use the same mix as for Vanilla Soufflé, adding the finely chopped zest of two lemons in place of the Vanilla. Three parts fill small buttered dariole moulds with this mixture, bake in a hot oven and turn out on to a hot dish. Sauce over with sabayon. See page 123.

353 Pouding Soufflé à l'Ananas

Substitute small dice of fresh pineapple for the lemon zest or vanilla.

354 Kapuziner Mehlspeise

This sweet is made with pancakes of soufflé mixture sandwiched with red currant jelly. Smear the soufflé moulds with butter (do not grease them with melted butter) and pour a few drops of milk in the bottom. Have ready the pancake pans and spoon out the soufflé mix to about the diameter of the moulds. When they are brown on the underside turn them over and finish the cooking. Place a pancake in the bottom of the soufflé mould with a spoonful of red currant jelly on top of it. Cover this with another pancake, more jelly and so on; but do not fill the moulds completely. Leave room to put about ½ in. of meringue on top. Then bake in a moderate oven for a short time until the pudding rises about 1 in. above the mould. Dust with icing sugar and serve at once.

NOTE ON THE SERVICE OF SOUFFLÉS

NEVER, repeat NEVER, use a knife to attempt to cut a soufflé into portions. NEVER dig into it with a tablespoon as though it were a rice pudding. Use two table forks back to back and lever it carefully apart into portions. Lift these on to the guest plates with a spoon and fork. You will perhaps never know the amount of work and skill that the craftsman has put into the making of that dish for you—respect it and enjoy your soufflé in perfection.

SAVOURIES

Though many may hold them to be gastronomically incorrect, savouries have probably come down to us from the times when our long-drinking forbears felt they needed something in the nature of an urge, l'Éperon Bachique, or a spicy something as an excuse for that last or penultimate bottle. Compare, in passing, the procedure across the Channel. In Normandy half-way through a celebration one drinks at a draught a glass of Apple Jack—you will not find any Calvados of equal strength over here—to make a hole in your stomach, *le trou Normand*, so that you can take more food on board!

355 Pavés au Fromage

Roll out puff pastry $\frac{3}{16}$ in. thick and from it cut two strips 4 in. wide. Mix together grated cheese and a saltspoonful of dry mustard. Make this into a paste with white of egg, spread it over one of the strips and place the other one carefully over it, making a sandwich. Press lightly. Wash the top surface with beaten egg and sprinkle sparsely with grated Parmesan cheese. Cut into $1\frac{1}{4}$-in. fingers and bake in a moderate oven.

356 Frozen Cream Cheese

Hang up to drain all sour milk and cream. When it is sufficiently dry, mix it well together adding a little fine salt, and if desired, a pinch of caraway seeds either whole or ground. Make into little parcels, wrapping them in nasturtium leaves secured with a cherry stick, and put in the refrigerator until frozen.

Selection of Savouries

top:
Croûtes Derby

left:
Shrimp Fritters

right:
Champignons á ma façon

centre:
Frozen Cream Cheese

bottom left:
Canapés Radjah

bottom right:
Swedish Savoury

357 Fried Cheese Sandwich

Grate finely any ends of cheese, season with dry mustard (cheese is already salted) and make into a paste with beaten egg. Spread this paste rather thickly on a slice of bread and cover with another slice. Trim off the crusts and cut the sandwich into four. Fry on both sides in oil.

358 Croque Monsieur

This is similar to the last. Spread the cheese mixture on both slices of bread and put a thin slice of cooked lean ham between them. Fry as before. It will probably be noticed that the cheese and egg mixture tends to souffler a little. This is an advantage and the savouries should be cooked as near as possible to the moment they will be required.

359 Welsh Rarebit

Crumble the cheese, or if hard and dry chop it. Melt it slowly with a little beer to help and when all lumps have disappeared season with a shake of Cayenne pepper and bind with a yolk of egg, stirring briskly. Pour on to toast and brown under the salamander.

360 Yorkshire Rarebit

Cut rings ¼-in. thick through the centre of an apple, leaving the skin on but removing the core. Cook these rings gently in a little butter and mount them on rounds of toasted bread; then pour Welsh rarebit over the top and gratinate.

361 Champignons sur Croûtes

If you have fresh incurved mushrooms at your disposal, wipe them clear of soil or other impurities, trim the ends of the stalks level with the rims of the mushrooms and cook them in butter with the addition of a little edible oil. Mount them on rounds of buttered toast and serve.

362 Champignons sur Croûtes (2)

If your mushrooms are showing signs of staleness, it is better to slice or chop them, cook them in butter then bind with a thick Béchamel sauce, highly seasoned. Spread this on toast giving it a domed appearance and allow to cool. When required for service, dip the prepared toasts in egg beaten with a *little* milk, pass them through fine breadcrumbs and fry in deep oil.

363 Champignons à ma Façon

Select incurved mushrooms of a good size and remove stalks. Chop these roughly and mix with an equal amount of diced boiled ham and fry together. Fill the mushrooms with this mixture, place a slice of tomato over and a small pat of butter, sprinkle with grated cheese and cook in the oven. On withdrawing place a black olive in the centre, and mount on a round of toast.

364 Canapé Fédora

Place a grilled mushroom on a toasted or fried canapé and fill the centre with pieces of grilled streaky bacon. Place a stuffed olive on top.

365 Canapés Epicure

Make a mixture of equal parts of Roquefort cheese, fresh butter and chopped dried walnuts. Spread this on the canapés. Serve cold.

366 Canapés Hollandais

If there is an odd piece or two of Findon haddock left over from the service at breakfast, remove the skin and bones carefully and either flake the fish small or chop it. Mix with lightly scrambled eggs, heighten the seasoning and spread the mixture on buttered toast. Cut into fingers and serve hot.

367 Canapé Diane

There are several ways of making this savoury, but you will find that the most practical is to roll the pieces of chicken livers separately in thin slices of streaky bacon, skewer them in position and cook them in the oven. De-skewer them, mount them on buttered pieces of toast, and just before serving, given them a touch with the glaze brush.

368 Brochettes de Foies de Volaille

This is identical with the last, except that two pieces of chicken liver alternating with thin pieces of streaky bacon are placed on each skewer; and the skewers are not removed after cooking. Serve on fingers of buttered toast.

369 Canapé Radjah

Pass some boiled ham trimmings through the fine plate of a mincer and make into a paste with cream. Spread this thickly on slices of toast, cover with a layer of chopped chutney (a hot variety) and sprinkle with grated cheese. Warm the toasts through in the oven and on removing them cut off the crusts, cut the slices into four and, if necessary, pop the canapés under the salamander for a moment to brown.

370 Bengal Toasts

Prepare as above, adding a little curry powder to the ham and cream mixture.

371 Beignets à la Mathurine

Make a small amount of pâte à choux, without sugar but seasoned with a little salt and cayenne pepper. Skin and bone some sardines and cut or break them in pieces. Chop a few anchovy fillets and mix all together. Next cut some pieces of grease-proof paper a little less in size than the top of your deep fat fryer, dip them in the fat and put them in a cool place. On these pieces of paper, using a teaspoon, put small heaps of the prepared pâte à choux. When the savouries are wanted, the papers are reversed on to the hot frying fat—the help of an assistant may be needed here—the little soufflés will free themselves and the papers may be removed and stored for the next time. Three to five of the beignets constitute a portion.

372 Beignets au Fromage

Substitute grated cheese for the sardine and anchovy in the above and proceed in the same way.

373 Cromesquis (with liver pâté)

Cut pieces of liver pâté 1½ in. square and ½ in. thick. Wrap them in thin pancakes, sealing well with beaten egg. They may then be dipped in a light frying batter and cooked in the deep fat, or passed through beaten egg and fine breadcrumbs before frying. The wrapping in thin pancakes is essential.

374 Swedish Savoury

Chop a hard-boiled egg not too finely, mix with it a finely chopped slice of onion which has been allowed to fall in butter and a chopped fillet of anchovy. Pile this mixture on a slice of buttered toast, cut into two, three or four according to size wanted, and put a ring of red pimento on top of each.

375 Scotch Woodcock

Pile scrambled egg on a slice of anchovy toast and smooth with a palette knife. Run trimmed fillets of anchovy from corner to corner. Where the fillets cross in the middle, a ring of anchovy may be made and filled with capers.

376 Croûtes Derby

Make a purée of unwanted scraps of cooked York ham by passing them through the fine plate of the mincer—a small proportion of ham fat may be incorporated. Make this into a workable paste by mixing it with double cream. Season with cayenne pepper and build up into domes on buttered toasts. Heat in the oven and, as garnish, place half a pickled walnut on top of each.

377 Herring Roes on Toast

Cook the soft herring roes slowly in butter. Arrange them on buttered fingers of toast. Sprinkle lightly with cayenne pepper, give them a squeeze of lemon juice, heat up the cooking butter and sauce the roes with it. Dust a little chopped parsley over when serving.

378 Craigie's Toast

Chop the flesh of a skinned and de-seeded tomato and allow it to fall in butter. Mix this with scrambled egg and heighten the seasoning. Spread the mixture on slices of buttered toast, remove the crusts and cut into four.

379 Shrimp Fritters

Wash a handful of picked shrimps and make sure that there are no stray bits of shell or feelers among them. Mix them into a light batter—one in which 2 whisked whites of egg have been incorporated—and drop ½ teaspoonful of this mixture into the deep fat fryer. Take them out with the spider when cooked, and drain them on absorbent paper. Dish on lace d'oyleys and serve with sections of lemon and a sprig of parsley. Have ready a boat of Rémoulade Sauce in case it is asked for.

SAUCES

380 Mayonnaise Sauce

In these days when nearly everyone possesses a liquidizer (coloquially known as a whizzer) the making of Mayonnaise Sauce is the matter of a few moments. Gone are the days when the youngest apprentice in the larder spent the whole morning turning 25 yolks into a bowlful, with the expenditure of much energy. In 30 seconds you can turn 1 whole egg—the white may be included unless you are collecting them for a batch of meringues or macaroons—1 tablespoon of wine vinegar, a pinch of salt, a turn of the pepper mill and ½ pint of oil into a mayonnaise that 'you could dance on'.

381 Sauce Rémoulade

To make the above Mayonnaise into a Sauce Rémoulade add to it 2 oz. pickled gherkins and 1 oz. of capers chopped together and pressed to remove moisture, a good pinch of chopped fines herbes (parsley, tarragon and chervil), a teaspoonful of essence of anchovies, and a good teaspoonful of French mustard.

382 Sauce Tartare

There seems to be some confusion in the minds of present day cooks concerning the two sauces, Rémoulade and Tartare. The former is prepared as above, the latter is a mayonnaise made from cooked yolks of egg. This is not so easy to make as an ordinary mayonnaise. Break down the yolks of 2 hard-boiled eggs into a paste with vinegar. When this is smooth add the oil in a thin stream, stirring briskly, and continue as for an ordinary mayonnaise. The garnish may consist simply of finely chopped chives or pounded green onion sieved, mixed with mayonnaise and added to the sauce. The addition of capers and gherkin is excluded as this is apt to confound Sauce Tartare with Sauce Rémoulade.

383 Sauce Gribiche

Make the sauce as above with yolks of hard-boiled eggs, oil, vinegar, made mustard, and seasoning as for mayonnaise, adding at the end chopped gherkins, capers, fines herbes and a julienne of cooked white of egg.

384 Sauce Fenouil Provençale

Make a Sauce Provençale by cooking chopped de-seeded tomatoes in very hot oil. Add a crushed clove of garlic, season with salt, pepper and a pinch of sugar. When the tomatoes are quite cooked mix with them a handful of stripped and chopped fennel. Thin if required with tomato sauce; remove the clove of garlic.

385 Tomato Sauce

Cut an onion and an equivalent amount of carrot into dice. Allow these to fry lightly in oil then add 2 tablespoonsful of flour and make into a roux. Use a 2½ size tin of tomato purée. See Sauce Portugaise—page 50, if fresh tomatoes are available. Add second stock to make up to desired quantity, season with pepper, salt and sugar, bring to the boil and cook either on the stove or covered in the oven until quite cooked and reduced. Strain through a pointed strainer and clear away in a basin. A few tiny pats of butter should be distributed over the sauce or a well-buttered round of a grease-proof paper placed on top, to stop the formation of skin.

386 Sauce Robert

Chop onions finely, allow them to cook in butter without

browning, add white wine and half the amount in wine vinegar, reduce, then add sauce demi-glace and lastly a spoonful of French mustard.

387 Sauce Poivrade

Cut a small mirepoix of 5 parts carrot, 4 parts onion, 4 parts celery, a few parsley stalks, a twig of thyme, a bayleaf, and a few crushed peppercorns. Fry these in oil until the vegetables have a light brown colour, drain, then add 2 parts of marinade and 1 part of wine vinegar. (It is assumed that the meat for which this sauce is intended has been marinaded in the usual way.) Reduce, then add twice the amount of sauce demi-glace. Continue the cooking for a further 20 minutes, then strain with pressure and bring the sauce to the desired consistency by the addition of marinade.

388 Sauce Hollandaise

Crush 8 peppercorns and reduce with a tablespoonful of wine vinegar in a sauteuse, adding when necessary a spoonful of water. Conduct this reduction on the corner of the stove, then put the sauteuse in a larger one containing hot water so that your further operations are conducted *en bain marie*. Add 4 yolks of egg and a spoonful of water, whisk until the egg yolks show signs of thickening then add 12 oz. of melted butter slowly, whisking the while. Season with salt and pepper (if needed).

Strain through two or three folds of muslin by twisting, to remove the broken peppercorns. This operation needs two persons. Freshly ground pepper from a pepper-mill may replace the crushed peppercorns, and the need for straining.

389 Sauce Madère

Reduce sufficient sauce demi-glace by one-quarter of its volume, keeping the spatula well pressed down to prevent sticking to the pan. Then add, off the fire, a glass of Madeira to bring the sauce back to its normal consistency.

390 Sauce Suprême

Reduce velouté of chicken with mushroom liquor until desired consistency is attained and strain by twisting through a tammy cloth. Finish with cream.

391 Sauce Villeroi

This sauce, serving as it does to mask objects destined to be fried in deep fat, is a well-reduced velouté bound with yolks. It is used for:

(*a*) Pieces of cold cooked chicken, boned breasts (six pieces), boned thighs (four pieces) and legs (two pieces).

(*b*) Quarter-inch slices of cooked sweetbreads.

(*c*) Short skewers of cooked lambs' breads.

(*d*) Lamb cutlets when braised in the piece can, when cold, be cut, trimmed and coated with Sauce Villeroi.

The subsequent treatment is either coating with a light frying batter or egg and breadcrumbing. The pieces are then fried in deep fat.

392 Sauce Vinaigrette

Measure 5 parts of olive oil and 2 parts of vinegar (French wine vinegar for preference), but most definitely NOT malt vinegar. To this add chopped parsley and an equal amount of chopped chervil, tarragon and chives. Pepper and salt to season.

For *Sauce Ravigote*, add to the above a spoonful of smallest capers and the same amount of very finely chopped shallots.

393 Sauce Vin Blanc

First you must make a *Fumet de Poisson*, i.e. a fish stock. Take

1 lb. of white fish bones and trimmings (skin, etc.). Butter the bottom of a saucepan and put in a thinly sliced onion with a crushed root of parsley or a few stalks. On this lay the fish bones and trimmings, squeeze the juice of half a lemon over, and cover the saucepan with its lid. Put this on the stove and allow to 'sweat'. Then pour over a quart of cold water, bring to the boil, skim and simmer for half an hour before straining, preferably through muslin.

The next step is to make a *Fish Velouté*. For this take 1 oz. of butter, make into a roux with 1 oz. of flour, then whisk in ¾ pint of the fumet. Continue boiling until reduced to ½ pint.

The last step is to take this ½ pint of velouté together with 2 spoonsful of white wine and bind it off the fire with 2 egg yolks and a tablespoonful of cream whisked together. Add a pat of butter then strain by forcing it with the back of a spoon through a fine strainer.

394 Beurre Maître d'Hôtel

Mix into softened butter chopped fines herbes (parsley, tarragon and chervil) and mix in a squeeze of lemon juice together with a pinch of cayenne pepper and salt if needed. Make into a roll in grease-proof paper which should be kept in the refrigerator—a round may then be cut off as required.

SWEET SAUCES

See Index.

MISCELLANEA

395 Wholemeal Bread

3 lb. Allinsons Wholemeal Flour
½ lb. White flour (plain)
1 oz. Salt
1 oz. Sugar
2 oz. Lard or Fat
2 oz. Yeast
2 pints Water

Mix flours, salt and sugar together and rub in the fat, then put the bowl in a warm place. It is best to put it over a pan of boiling water, stir the mixture about and when it feels warm to the hand, remove from the heat. Dissolve the yeast in part of the water, which should be at blood-heat; then make into a dough with all the liquid and dry ingredients. Divide this dough into three parts and mould it to fit three 2-lb. bread tins. Allow it to prove until it fills the tins, then bake for 1 hour in a temperature of 400° F. On withdrawing from the oven take the loaves from the tins to prevent the steam from softening the crust.

396 Baps and Breakfast Rolls (Wholemeal)

These may be made from the above dough. Baps or breakfast rolls are weighed at 6 oz. for four. The dough is rolled into a ball and, on recovery from this, pinned with a rolling pin to a disc 6 in. in diameter. This is cut into four and the pieces placed on a greased and warmed baking sheet which is then put into a proving oven or prover. As it is unlikely that any but a large hotel will have a bakery attached, an improvised prover may be made by using a warm oven. It must be remembered that yeast works best at a temperature of about 90° F., so verify that the heat of the prover is kept low. When the dough has risen to about twice the size, bake the baps in a hot oven.

For Breakfast or Finger rolls, weigh at 4 oz. for four, pin out as above, cut into four. Roll the pieces into little balls then roll under the hand into finger shapes. Put them as before on to greased and warmed baking sheets then into the prover. When the rolls are roughly double the size, wash them over with a soft brush dipped in milk—to give them a slight glaze—and bake in a hot oven.

Allinson's Wholemeal Flour is mentioned in the above recipe because it is the only one that I know milled from whole wheat between stones in the old-fashioned way. There may be others up and down the country.

397 Scones

1 lb. Flour
2 oz. Sugar
1½ oz. Baking Powder
2 oz. Margarine
1 Egg
½ pint (scant) Milk

Sieve the flour and baking powder together on to the slab or table and rub in fat, make a bay, add the egg, sugar and the milk. Make into a light dough without any toughening. Flour the table and pat out this dough to the thickness of about ¾ inch. From this cut the scones with a 2-in. diameter round cutter. Place them on a greased baking-sheet and bake in a hot oven as near 500° F. as you can get it.

398 Genoese

Our electric ovens were large, the baking sheets measured about 20 in. × 24 in. and were turned up 1 in. on all four sides. Admirable for baking a slab of Genoese. We used the following quantities for this size, but they can be adjusted proportionately.

1½ lb Butter
1½ lb. Caster Sugar
1 lb. 14 oz. Eggs in shell
1 lb. 14 oz. Flour, sieved with
1 oz. Baking Powder

Put the softened butter with the sugar into the cake machine and beat into a cream, then add the eggs slowly beating between additions until a light batter is obtained. Remove the beater and get an assistant to shake the flour into the bowl whilst you stir it in carefully by hand. Take care not to overmix. Meantime have a baking sheet papered with a sheet of greaseproof paper and turn the mixture out on to it, spreading it evenly. Bake in a temperature of 380° F.

399 Chocolate Genoese

Use the above recipe and method, substituting 6 oz. cocoa for 6 oz. of the flour.

400 Victoria Sponge

Beat 1 lb. 10 oz. fine sugar and 1 pint eggs in the machine until light, then add 10 oz. water (½ pint) in which you have dissolved 1 oz. of glycerine. Lastly stir in carefully 1 lb. 9 oz. flour into which you have sieved 2 oz. of baking powder and 1 oz. dried milk.

This mixture should then be divided into sandwich pans (6 in. in diameter with a paper circle in the bottom). It will make sixteen to eighteen, or some of the mixture can be poured on to a paper-lined sheet tin and smoothed out into a rectangle, baked and kept in reserve as bases for ices or iced sweets.

401 Shortbread

Weigh ½ lb. caster sugar and 1 lb. slightly softened butter into the bowl of the mixing machine and cream together. Sieve together 1 lb. flour, ¼ lb. rice flour and ¼ lb. cornflour, add these to creamed butter and sugar in the machine and mix all into a firm dough. Paper a baking sheet with grease-proof paper and extend the above dough on it to the thickness of ¼ in. Trim the ragged edges leaving a rectangle which you cut into bands 3 in. in width. Then cut the bands into fingers 1¼ in. wide. Leave all in position on the paper for the baking. The temperature of the oven should be 380° F. or thereabouts.

402 Baking Powder

Mix well together ¼ lb. bicarbonate of soda, ½ lb. cream of tartar and ¾ lb. rice flour or cornflour (or proportionately for smaller quantities). Put this mixture through a fine sieve twice and store in an airtight tin. You will get better results if you use this mix in preference to ready-made baking powder.

Many bought ready-made baking powders contain tartaric acid, which acts on the bi-carbonate of soda when they are mixed with water in the cold. The evolution of gas is too rapid and the reaction spent before the goods are ready for the oven. This difficulty is overcome by the substitution of cream of tartar for the free acid. The action does not occur until heat is applied, thus giving more time for recovery from toughening in the dough.

403 Crème au Beurre

Use twice as much sugar (icing or fine caster) as butter (say 1 lb. sugar to ½ lb. butter). Beat this up well. Flavour the mixture according to your requirements, transfer to a basin and keep covered with a paper in the refrigerator.

404 Cream

If you use much cream it may be to your advantage to buy yourself a small cream-making machine. This emulsifies milk and oiled fresh (unsalted) butter into cream, which may be used fresh or purposely soured by the careful addition of a little lemon juice or vinegar. Use ¾ lb. unsalted butter to 1 pint milk. Melt the butter in a small quantity of the milk and use the remainder to reduce the temperature to roughly blood heat. If the cream does not 'make' first time through (a degree or two too much heat will cause this), pump it through again. You will soon get the knack of it.

405 Orange Marmalade

During the time I was the lessee of the Fortingall Hotel, about thirty-four years, we always made our own Orange Marmalade, rising at the end to a quarter of a ton every spring.

3¾ lb. Seville Oranges
Juice of 4 Lemons
9 pints Water
9 lb. Sugar

Halve the oranges and squeeze out the juice. Soak the pips in 1 pint of the water. Shread the orange caps on a marmalade-cutting machine, and soak them in the remainder of the water. Next day put the shredded peel with the water on to boil and when it is cooked add the sugar, orange and lemon juice and the water in which the pips have been soaking. Boil to 218° F. and clear away in 7-lb. jam jars. Next day put a circle of grease-proof paper on top of the marmalade and tie a piece of brown paper over the mouth of each jar. It is necessary to put the date on this paper.

The lemon caps need not be wasted, they may be made into lemon peel.

406 Lemon peel

Having soaked the lemon caps in cold water for a few hours, remove the remains of the segments from the interiors and boil in slightly salted water until tender. Afterwards allow the cold water tap to run over them for several hours. Then drain them and immerse them in a syrup of 4 lb. sugar to 2½ pints water, more or less but in that proportion, and bring to the boil. Pour into a jam jar and put away until next day.

Then next day drain off the syrup, bring it to the boil, add a little more sugar. This is the most difficult part of the whole operation as without the necessary testing instruments one can only guess the amount of sugar required. The object is to bring back the syrup to the same strength as on the first day. When this is done put in the peel again and bring to the boil. Then clear away in a jam jar until next day and continue this operation for 3 or 4 days. At the end of this time the peel will be impregnated with sugar syrup and will have the familiar clear look. It may be stored in its own syrup or drained and chopped.

The syrup may be used again and again. Simply add more sugar and water if required to obtain the necessary strength and quantity. Do not have the syrup too dense or the peel will harden, i.e. it will give up moisture and not take up sugar syrup in exchange.

If desired the peel, when finished, may be put through the mincer and the stock of syrup stored away for the next time—it will keep.

407 Orange Peel

Caps of orange peel may be dealt with in the same manner.

Pralin

See page 129.

408 To pickle pork

Those earthenware cruchons, which our mothers used for pickling eggs or salting butter in days not so long ago, are the very thing. The quantities required for the pickling of meat are:

½ gallon of Water
1 lb. Coarse Salt
4 oz. Brown Sugar
¼ oz. Saltpetre.

These are boiled together and allowed to cool before the meat is immersed. Leave in pickle for at least 3 days. In fact the pickle will keep for months if boiled occasionally: it is a recipe for sugar-cured meat from Yorkshire.

---

409 Soap

It is a good plan to turn some, if not all, of the surplus waste fat that accumulates in the kitchen into soap. Melt 6 lb. of the fat and strain it. Dissolve a 1 lb. tin of caustic soda in 1½ pints of water. Have ready a small wooden box lined with pieces of old sheeting for which you have no further use. Soak this material in cold water before lining the box which should stand on a level baking-tin. Next mix the dissolved caustic and melted fat together, stirring carefully to avoid splashes on hands or face, and pour the mixture into the prepared box. Allow to stand until the next day, then cut into bars and ultimately into pieces which you should store in a dry place to harden. Make certain that no salty fat, such as bacon or ham is used, or the soap will not set.

GLOSSARY

Bain Marie. A water-bath to keep hot soups, sauces and the like.

Beurre Manié. Equal weights of softened butter and sieved flour mixed together and used to thicken or bind sauces, etc. Whisked in.

Bouquet Garni. A few parsley stalks or a green leaf of leek, a bay leaf and a branch of dried thyme made into a little bundle by tying with a piece of string. The bouquet is used to flavour a stew of meat, etc. If the string is left long it may be tied to the handle of the pan to facilitate withdrawal at any time.

Brunoise. Very small dice of vegetables easily formed by cutting a julienne into tiny cubes (carrot, celery, turnip and leek).

Grosse Brunoise. Is the same but about ¼-in. sides, carrot, turnip, onion and perhaps potato. Used as a garnish for certain meat entrées.

Bouquets. The dressing of a garnish or salad in small neat heaps.

Casserole. Copper pans of varying sizes used in a kitchen. Or earthenware dishes oval or round with lids, used to cook or to serve.

Ciseler. To make small cuts on each side of the back of a fish to help in the cooking. To cut a vegetable into fine shreds.

Concasser. To chop roughly.

Cornichons. Gherkins pickled in vinegar.

Cuisson. The act of cooking, or the stock, etc., in which the cooking took place.

Déglaçage. When a piece (or several small pieces) of meat, fish, poultry or game have been braised, the congealed juices are found on the pan in the form of a glaze. This is an essence and should be dissolved in wine or stock and added to the final sauce.

Émincer. To cut a fruit or vegetable into very thin slices.

Fall, to. A short preliminary cooking of vegetables in oil or fat of some kind, to render them limp and in some cases to allow them to take colour slightly.

Fond Blanc. If, after the clarification of a consommé, the marmite is refilled with water, brought to the boil and kept steadily boiling for a few hours, a second stock will be produced known as fond blanc. It is useful for the making of thick soups, sauces or the poaching of chicken.

Frissoner. Literally 'to shiver'. To allow a liquid to come nearly to the boil—to simmer.

Glaze. See Déglaçage above. Surplus stock is sometimes reduced by boiling to the state of a thick brown syrup. It is hoarded like gold, for it is invaluable for the enrichment of clear soups, brown sauces and gravies.

Gros Sel. Is just coarse salt or freezing salt.

Julienne. A cut of vegetables, carrot, turnip, celery, leek, the length of a match but thinner, used as a garnish in consommé. A julienne of chicken, ham or tongue is sometimes called for but is more rubust in proportions.

Jus de Veau Lié. Veal stock reduced by boiling and thickened if necessary with arrowroot.

Lardoir. A large-sized larding needle used to insert lardoons through a chunky piece of rump of beef as for Boeuf à la Mode.

Lardoon. A ⅜-in. square section length of larding bacon inserted in a piece of beef for braising. The bacon should be long enough to pass through the meat in the sense of the grain. It is best to insert the lengths 1 in. apart about 1 in. in from the outer edge.

Larding-needle. Not to be confused with the above. This is a hollow needle about 6 in. long with the end opposite the point, having four 'leaves' to grip a strip of larding bacon about 2 in. long and $\frac{3}{16}$ in. square section which is 'sewn' into a fold of a fillet of beef, a filet mignon or a sweetbread leaving ¼ in. of the bacon showing at each end. Rows of these insertions may be made into a herring-bone pattern.

Mandoline. A knife set at an angle in an adjustable board which enables one to slice vegetables in varying thicknesses. A serrated knife blade makes lattice slices of potatoes possible by moving the potato between cuts to a different angle.

Mijouter. To cook gently, to simmer.

Mirepoix. Dice of carrots, onion, celery, with a little thyme and a fragment of bay leaf and dice of raw ham or blanched belly pork allowed to cook together slowly in fat and used to augment flavour of meats, fish, shellfish, etc.

Oignon Brulé. A roasted onion—one put into the kitchen fire among the glowing cinders for a few minutes and transferred to a stock to give flavour and colour. Nowadays the onion is halved and the cut side put down on the electric hot-plate.

Petit Salé. Home brine-cured flank of pork.

Plat à Poisson. An oval dish used for the cooking of fish; say a whole sole.

Poêle à Omelette. An omelette pan.

Pointe de Cayenne. As much as will stay on ½ in. at the end of a small kitchen knife when plunged into a heap of cayenne pepper.

Poivrons. The French word for Green Pepper, Capsicum or Pimento.

Rafraîchir. The act of cooling under running water a meat, fish or vegetable which has been brought to the boil from cold.

Ravier. A small oval or diamond-shaped dish used for salads or hors d'oeuvre.

Salamander. Nowadays an electric or gas grill, formerly a thick piece of cast iron which was heated to bright red in the kitchen fire and used to 'glacer' various dishes.

Sauteuse. A shallow pan with sloping sides in which it is easy to toss the contents.

Le Sot l'y Laisse. 'The fool leaves it there.' Two muscles about the size of the top joint of one's thumb found under the skin on each side of the pelvic bone in a roast chicken carcase. Known here as 'the oyster'.

Spider. The name given to a flat curl of wire (sometimes 'dished' slightly) on a long handle used for removing elements which are being fried in the deep fat.

Tomates Concassées. Tomatoes, skinned, seeded and roughly chopped. Allowed to fall in butter. Seasoned with pepper, salt, and a pinch of sugar.

Turned vegetables. Pieces of carrot and turnip ¾ in. long as garnish for Pot-au-Feu or Petit Marmite and 2 in. long for Navarin de Mouton, Boiled gigot of Mutton, Boiled Beef and the like. The edges of the pieces are taken off the vegetables making them like little six-sided barrels.

Skillet. A name given to a frying-pan in America; but over here it signifies a sugar-boiler's untinned copper pan, furnished with a spout at one side and a socket into which a short length of broom shaft may be driven to act as a handle.

INDEX

NOTE – Figures in **bold** type are the relevant recipe numbers, and figures in roman type the page references.

INDEX